AUGUST WILSON
AND THE
AFRICAN-AMERICAN
ODYSSEY

KIM PEREIRA

UNIVERSITY OF ILLINOIS PRESS

URBANA AND CHICAGO

Illini Books edition, 1995
© 1995 by the Board of Trustees of the University of Illinois
Manufactured in the United States of America
1 2 3 4 5 C P 5 4 3 2

This book is printed on acid-free paper.

Library of Congress Cataloging-in-Publication Data

Pereira, Kim, 1952–
    August Wilson and the African-American odyssey / Kim Pereira.
        p.   cm.
    Includes bibliographical references (p.   ) and index.
    ISBN 0-252-02137-1 (acid-free paper). — ISBN 0-252-06429-1 (pbk. :
acid-free paper)
    1. Wilson, August—Criticism and interpretation. 2. Historical
drama, American—History and criticism. 3. Domestic drama,
American—History and criticism. 4. Afro-American families in
literature. 5. Afro-Americans in literature. 6. Family in
literature. I. Title.
PS3573.I45677Z83   1995
812'.54—dc20   94-25855
                                                        CIP

For Lorraine
who put her dreams on hold to help me follow mine

CONTENTS

PREFACE

In 1984, the *New York Times* critic Frank Rich called August Wilson a "major find for the American Theatre." Within the next eight years, this endorsement was emphatically underscored as Wilson won Pulitzer Prizes (for *Fences* and *The Piano Lesson*), Antoinette Perry ("Tony") Awards, New York Drama Critics' Circle Awards, Drama Desk Awards, and several other theater accolades. His artistic goal of writing a play for every decade of the twentieth century promises to become a dramatic testament not only to the experiences of African Americans but to the history of all Americans.

After a childhood of poverty in Pittsburgh, Pennsylvania, a city that became the setting for many of his plays, Wilson quit school at the age of sixteen and began working at menial jobs, during which time he undoubtedly garnered insights into the black working class that later produced such rich characters as Troy Maxson, the garbage collector protagonist of *Fences,* and Boy Willie, the visionary in *The Piano Lesson.* Despite dropping out of school—an act partly prompted by the refusal of a history teacher to accept his word that his essay was not plagiarized—Wilson continued to pursue a literary career by successfully submitting poems to black publications at the University of Pittsburgh Press.

In 1968, Wilson founded the Black Horizons Theatre Company in St. Paul, Minnesota. There he wrote his first play, *Jitney,* a realistic drama set in a Pittsburgh taxi station. It was accepted for workshop production at the O'Neill Theatre Center's National Playwrights Conference in 1982 and was followed by another play, *Fullerton Street.* His reputation as an important playwright was secured only after his third play, *Ma Rainey's Black Bottom,* was produced at the Yale Repertory Theatre under the direction of Yale Drama School's artistic director, Lloyd Richards, who also directed several other plays by Wilson. This continuing partnership is probably one of the most fruitful artistic collaborations between playwright and director in the history of the American theater. Together, Richards and Wilson changed the face of the American theater and finally secured for African-American playwrights their rightful place in the national theater scene.

I was first drawn to Wilson's plays by the voice that spoke so intimately about an African-American odyssey, a voice that resounded among the traditions and mythologies of my own native India. In structuring his plays around the rituals, folklore, and music of Africans and African Americans, Wilson emphasizes the universal aspect of his work, for it would seem that in this fractured global society of the late twentieth century, the common threads of similarity between human beings lie buried among the lore and legends of the cultures of the world.

The stories of a community of people reinventing their cultural identity are as universal as the tales of Native Americans or the legends of India or the political struggles of South Africans, Israelis, Palestinians, the Irish, and the peoples of the former Soviet Union. Wilson's narratives have an urgency because they are a poetic apprehension of a history in the making—there is almost the feeling that his stories leap from the stage onto our streets, instead of the other way around.

In my journey through these plays there were many guiding lights who illuminated each step, and I would like to acknowledge their help. The members of my dissertation committee at Florida State University, and particularly my mentor, Dr. Stuart Baker, who, with his wife, Jalma, befriended me from the moment I landed on these shores; Bernard Peterson and Paul Carter Harrison, who read my manuscripts and, curbing their irritation at my naïveté, offered instead valuable suggestions that illuminated so many corners of the plays.

I could not have undertaken this project without the love of my wife, Lorraine, who helped in more ways than I can say; and my children, Liesl and Kieran, who literally hung about my neck as I typed the manuscript and are, therefore, woven into my work as they are into my life.

INTRODUCTION

The history of black Americans reveals a pattern of migration and separation, beginning with the great involuntary migration from Africa that separated a whole race of people from their homes and culture, thrusting them into a totally alien environment. This pattern continued throughout their incarceration, as black families were abruptly sundered and husbands, wives, and children flung far and wide among the great plantations of the South, where voluntary movement was curbed and blacks could not travel without a pass.

As described by Eric Foner, these forced migrations and restrictions on free movement created not only a deep social disruption among them but a spiritual dislocation that resulted in a flurry of movement once they were manumitted. "With emancipation, it seemed that half the South's black population took to the roads. 'Right off colored folks started on the move,' a Texas slave later recalled. 'They seemed to want to get closer to freedom, so they'd know what it was—like it was a place or a city'" (80). The movement of blacks after emancipation was a physical expression of a profound spiritual and social disquietude built up through the centuries of slavery. This restless wandering had its roots in the slave experience and was at the heart of every tale told from an African viewpoint (Stuckey 5). In the "King Buzzard Tale,"[1] for example, a wandering buzzard represents a traitorous tribal chieftain, but its metaphorical implications seem to include all enslaved Africans, the essential conclusion being that slavery leads to a destruction of spiritual moorings, resulting in restlessness.

Contrary to sociological expectations that forced migrations and their attendant spiritual anxiety would destroy any sense of familial obligation among them, former slaves strengthened their family ties by legalizing their marriage bonds or by adopting orphaned children rather than see them apprenticed to white masters (Foner 84). It is not surprising, therefore, that immediately after emancipation, the desire to travel was also spurred by the effort to reunite families. Foner regards this as the most "poignant . . . of all the motivations for black mobility" and reports that the Freedman's Bureau did not consider the work of emancipation complete "until the families which had been dispersed by slavery were reunited" (82).

The very process of familial disruption by slavery, according to Sterling Stuckey, engendered a larger, communal affinity among blacks linked by the collective bond of their suffering and the commonality of their African past. "The final gift of African 'tribalism' in the nineteenth century was its life as a lingering memory in the minds of American slaves. That memory enabled them to go back to the sense of community in the traditional African setting and to include all Africans in their common experience of oppression in North America" (3). Although slavery was dehumanizing and deleterious to the preservation of a sense of community and resulted in fracturing communal bonds among the slaves, it was never able to shatter them completely (Levine 33). The migration of blacks can therefore be viewed not only as an attempt to find lost family members but, by extension, as a yearning to return to the lost community from which they were originally severed. Into this pattern of separation and migration a third theme thus entered the rhythm of the lives of these ex-slaves—that of reunion.

In his plays examined in this study, August Wilson deals with the effects of separation, migration, and reunion on the descendants of slaves who migrated from the rural South to the urban North. After Reconstruction failed to vindicate, in any practical terms, their dreams of being accepted as equal partners in the new society of the post–Civil War South, their proclivity for traveling became a dire practical necessity as they sought refuge in such northern cities as Chicago, Philadelphia, Pittsburgh, and New York. This new migration naturally involved separation from the past, from their families and the "downhome familiar" (the smells, sights, and sounds) of life back home in the Deep South. In examining the lives of these migrant blacks, Wilson's focus is on their dreams, their restlessness, and their struggle to find practical and spiritual havens in an essentially hostile society. His examination of these aspects of the lives of his characters also raises interesting questions about the rural South and the black American's place in it, and he explores the decisions that led them away from the familiarity of their farms into a strange industrial milieu.

Since reunion with lost family members was not always possible in a country so vast, Wilson elevates this theme to a new, mystical dimension by suggesting that black migration is ultimately a quest for self-authentication and empowerment. Therefore, his characters cannot be defined within the narrow framework of the social roles they are forced to accept in an inimical society, for they are seeking spiritual unification with the mythological aspects of their greater cultural identity as Africans. In *Joe Turner's Come and Gone,* Loomis searches for and finds his African self. This theme, with a number of variations, explains the actions of many other characters in Wilson's plays.

In his afterword to *August Wilson: Three Plays*, Paul Carter Harrison draws an interesting connection between Levee (*Ma Rainey*), Troy Maxson (*Fences*), Herald Loomis (*Joe Turner*), and the Yoruba trickster deity, Eshu. "He is the mythic hero as underdog, the trickster legacy of Yoruba mythology, Eshu—reinvented throughout the diaspora as Exu in Brazil, Elegua in Cuba, Papa Legba in Haiti, and the Signifyin' Monkey in urban black America—who mediates the obstacles that threaten survival and harmony with wit, cunning, guile, and a godly sense of self-empowerment which accords him extravagant transgressions. Alogical and nontraditional—at least more adept at improvisation—he is unimpressed with social constraints established for mortals of average size" (301–2). By tracing the mythological ancestry of these characters to Eshu, Harrison focuses attention on the cosmological dimension of Wilson's plays as it intersects with the mundane struggles of his characters.

That this spiritual and religious spectrum is an integral part of the lives of blacks—indeed, that it cannot really be isolated from the "material" aspects—has long been accepted by historians. It is a characteristic common not only to the peoples of Africa but throughout the Eastern hemisphere.[2] The alignment of the material world with the divine stems from the fact that "when [Africans] looked upon the cosmos they saw Man, Nature, and God as a unity; distinct but inseparable aspects of a sacred whole" (Levine 32). This universal perspective dominates Wilson's plays as ghosts, divine revelations, and spirits easily and naturally interact with the world of common experience.

The themes of separation, migration, and reunion are central to Wilson's exploration of the search by blacks for cultural identity and self-affirmation. Though the actual migration has already taken place at the time of some of the plays, it is still a dominant theme, for its effects continue to shape the lives of the characters.

In *Ma Rainey's Black Bottom,* for example, separation and migration are manifested through stories and reminiscences as a group of black musicians learn the cost of preserving the integrity of the musical traditions that are beginning to define them.

In Wilson's next play, *Fences,* the theme of separation is further explored. *Fences* is the tale of Troy Maxson—the embittered son of a sharecropper—and his struggle to cope with the winds of change sweeping the country in the late fifties. Having migrated north after escaping from a violent father, Troy finds himself in a similar predicament with his son Cory, with the roles now reversed. The play deals with the pain that psychological separation brings family members as each generation gropes toward reconciliation with the previous one.

While *Fences* explores themes in the lives of a number of characters, *Joe Turner's Come and Gone* is in large part the story of one tormented man looking for his estranged wife and the answers to his own identity. Mirroring his quest are a host of restless characters wandering up and down the country, ostensibly in search of lost relatives, old loves, and new relationships, but actually on a crusade of self-discovery.

Separation and reunion are again the main themes in *The Piano Lesson,* in which the central symbol, a relic of the past, becomes the nerve center of a conflict between siblings. Each of them invests the piano with a different meaning: to Berniece it is a sacrosanct heirloom; to her brother it is, at first, a piece of merchandise to be traded for his farm. Their conflict is an internal separation that must be exorcised to clear the way for spiritual reconciliation and reunion.

Pivotal to the theme of reunion in Wilson's plays is the underlying premise to which he constantly returns—that the solutions for the future lie in the past. Clues to the identity of black Americans are strewn along a cultural trail that leads backward through slavery all the way to Africa. Only in a spiritual communion with this rich heritage will blacks realize an understanding of their true worth. Some characters, like Cory in *Fences,* need a reunion with the immediate past: father and son must be reconciled. Some, like Loomis in *Joe Turner,* must probe deep within their racial unconscious to find the answers in Africa. But whatever the particulars, all the characters must, in one way or another, embrace the past, for it is only in their roots that they will discover their true identities. Those roots may lie in an ancient African tradition or in the more recent ethos of the American South.

Wilson's fifth play, *Two Trains Running,* set in a Pittsburgh diner in 1969, is not included in this study because the themes of separation, migration, and reunion—which form the unifying rhythms in the four earlier plays—are not integral to its structure. It appears to mark the beginning of a different set of plays in the post–civil rights era from the plays before the nineteen sixties. Only faint traces of the old themes linger as new ones emerge. The warrior spirit that marks Levee, Troy, and Boy Willie promises to explode across a greater gamut of characters as turbulent times call for severe solutions. The changing music in the final decades of the century, from soul to rap, will reflect a new kind of yearning, one with a brittle, violent edge.

By 1969, the migration north had long since ended, and the black characters in *Two Trains Running* are as much northerners as any white people. Although Memphis does talk about his land in Jackson, Mississippi, and how he lost it and how he means to go back for it someday, for the most part he and the other characters are busy working, hustling, and struggling to make a living in the urban North, their attention focused on the present and the future, with the past merely a distant memory.

But Wilson does not completely abandon his view of the healing power of the past. As though sensing that the cultural past is quickly receding beyond the reach of these people, he introduces a fascinating offstage character, Aunt Ester, who is a repository of all the struggles and victories of African Americans. This 349-year-old woman (as old as the presence of African Americans in America) is a cultural storehouse of memory and experience from whom the diseased and the disenchanted, the hopeful and the desperate may seek solutions and new direction. Hers is the oracular voice, authenticated by a collective unconscious and a racial memory, that sings healing hymns first whispered in an all-but-forgotten past.

Two Trains Running is Wilson's first post–civil rights play. The year 1969 was obviously an anxious time in the lives and fortunes of African Americans. The riots and conflagrations that surrounded the death of Martin Luther King, Jr., had left in their wake an uneasy social climate. At the beginning of this play, the characters are awaiting the funeral of one of the neighborhood residents. The death of the "Prophet Samuel," whose funeral arrangements are constantly referred to throughout the play, may be seen, on one level, as an extended metaphor for the temporary, symbolic death of the civil rights movement, for his death follows not long after the deaths of the leaders of the two extreme ends of the movement—Martin Luther King and Malcolm X. The struggle to survive appears to falter, if only for a moment—as the characters contemplate not only the death of the "prophet" but also the city council's renovation project that threatens to tear down their neighborhood—but by the end of the play the journey toward self-authentication continues along new paths through the new social terrain of the post–civil rights movement. This pause in the struggle is made even more poignant by the breakdown of the jukebox in the diner—the music that, for three centuries, helped black people through their darkest periods is now silenced, and, for a Wilson play, this silence is deafening. It is noteworthy that for much of the play Aunt Ester is ill and cannot admit visitors, a further reminder of the fragile link to the past. Thus, the music and the oracle, cultural conduits to the past, are temporarily inaccessible.

Two Trains Running reflects the complex social tapestry surrounding African Americans at the end of the sixties. Many of them no longer lived in abject poverty. There are several references to the trappings of commercial success—Cadillacs, color TVs, jewelry, even property. But there are far more references to crime, guns, and killings. Blacks are fighting back any way they can. Refusing to accept the settlement that the city offers him, Memphis goes to court and is astonished to receive a greater amount than he had expected. Unless they fight and take what is theirs, they are doomed to become like Hambone, who goes insane waiting for justice. Memphis runs a diner but finds his business slackening as the neighborhood starts to disintegrate—the supermarket, two drugstores, the doctor, and the dentist have all gone. "Ain't nothing gonna be left but these niggers killing one another," he says. West discovers the most lucrative job—burying other black people.

Despite the tumultuous times, the spirit of survival among Wilson's characters remains undiminished as they continue to scramble and hope—playing the lottery, stealing if they have to, and working where they can. By the end of the play, Sterling manages to see Aunt Ester, who offers him hope and the promise of love. That same day, the music returns—the jukebox is repaired and, even before Risa plays it, Sterling sings to her in a faltering prelude to the full-blown swells of Aretha Franklin's soulful voice. The odyssey continues.

In each of his plays, Wilson uses as his backdrop the social and political atmosphere of the decade under consideration. His excellent sense of history and firm grasp of the fluctuating social changes in the lives of black people throughout the course of the twentieth century enable him to capture the mood of the decade without resorting to mere commentary.

Although racial discrimination casts a shadow over all the plays, and prejudice and harassment are continually present, Wilson's primary objective is not to heap vehement blame on white America. As one of his characters in *Ma Rainey* says: "Now what's the colored man gonna do with himself? That's what we waiting to find out. . . . The problem ain't with the white man. The white man know you just a leftover. 'Cause he the one who done the eating and he know what he done ate. . . . Done went and filled the white man's belly and now he's full and tired and wants you to get out of the way and let him be by himself" (58). Wilson's focus is not so much on what black people were denied—though that is incalculable—but on what they possess: an indomitable spirit, a bottomless capacity for survival, and a rich sensibility informed by a music born in an ancient culture. With the exception of *Ma Rainey,* the tone of his plays is ultimately transcendent. His is a compassionate voice, probing, searching for possible solutions, sometimes reprimanding, but always feeling with his people as they strive to comprehend a society that keeps changing the rules as soon as they learn them.

Essential to an understanding of Wilson's plays is the importance of black music, and particularly the blues, which he acknowledges to be the wellspring of his art. In an interview with Bill Moyers, Wilson said that "the blues are important primarily because they contain the cultural responses of blacks in America to the situation that they find themselves in. Contained in the blues is a philosophical system at work. You get the ideas and attitudes of people as part of the oral tradition. That is a way of passing along information. . . . The music provides you an emotional reference for the information, and it is sanctioned by the community in the sense that if someone sings the song, other people sing the song" (14). In some instances, the blues is an integral part of the subject (*Ma Rainey*), and in others, it takes on a more symbolic role (*Piano Lesson*); but whatever the precise usage, its dramatic function reveals a black aesthetic of tragi-comic lyricism that endured despite—and indeed because of— the pitiless experiences of three and a half centuries.

The blues developed from African and African-American worksongs and sorrow songs. Field hollers, shouts, yells, and mournful spirituals provided the structural foundation for the growth of this music. As it took shape it began to reflect the emotional content of the lives of blacks—essentially, their struggle to deal with and rise above their depressed lifestyles. The blues thereby became a safety valve that permitted them to release the tension and pressure resulting from daily trials. The cathartic lyrics purged the anxiety brought on by separation, loneliness, and love affairs gone sour. The blues was the companion of many blacks. Wilson's Ma Rainey says that the blues "help you get out of bed in the morning. You get up knowing you ain't alone. There's something else in the world. You get up knowing whatever your troubles is you can get a grip on them 'cause the blues done give you an understanding of life." Although the blues might not possess the transcendent resolution of spirituals, it struck an emotional chord that resonated with hope even in the darkest moments. In *Shadow and Act,* Ralph Ellison's definition imbues the blues with a poetic aspect. "The Blues is an impulse to keep the painful details and episodes of a brutal experience alive in one's aching consciousness, to finger its jagged grain and to transcend it, not by the consolation of philosophy but by squeezing from it a near-tragic, near-comic lyricism. As a form, the blues is an autobiographical chronicle of personal catastrophe expressed lyrically" (78).

It is significant that the blues as we know it really came into its own during the turn of the century, at one of the worst periods in the modern history of black America. At that time, blacks were forced to realize that the freedom on which they had waited all their lives existed only in a legal document with little meaning in the real world. Only the Constitution was amended; little else changed. Attitudes and practices designed to keep them in an underprivileged position were the order of the day—sharecropping enslaved them on the plantation, and the "Separate but Equal" Supreme Court decision of 1896 segregated them in the social arena. It was at this bleak moment in their history that they created the blues. Just as the worksongs, hollers, and spirituals had helped them move beyond the despair of slavery, the deeply felt emotions of the blues now helped them transcend the angst that rose from freedom without opportunity.

These strong emotional overtones in the blues find varied expressions in Wilson's plays. In *Ma Rainey,* Levee's frustration at not being allowed to write a song his way reaches such a pitch that he kills one of his fellow musicians. In *Joe Turner,* this sense of the music being inextricably woven with the cultural identity of blacks is given symbolic shape as the characters search for their "song." Wilson says that in *Joe Turner* the "song" Loomis seeks is his African identity. "Understanding who you are . . . you can [then] go out and sing your song as an African" (Moyers 16). Or, as Bynum tells Loomis in the same play, "All you got to do is sing it. Then you be free." In finding his own song—his "African-ness," his roots—the African American discovers his own identity and the value of his true self.

If at first glance the plays appear to be as loosely structured as the lives of their characters, this form merely reflects the traditions of the people depicted. Wilson writes out of a black dramatic tradition that inspired such playwrights as Langston Hughes to incorporate into their works the structure of the blues, gospel music, black sermons, and storytelling. Closer examination of Wilson's plays reveals a complex rather than a loose form. Like a Shakespearean play, when viewed spatially instead of linearly, each of Wilson's plays unveils an intricate network of cross-referent motifs and images that creates a unique mood and atmosphere for each work. *Ma Rainey,* for instance, resembles a jazz composition. At the beginning, four musicians sit around chatting while they wait for Ma Rainey to arrive. One of them tells a story, then they go back to their conversations until the next story, and so on. Each story is like a solo performance in a jazz quartet that, though it possesses the characteristics of a "set piece," is related to the major themes on an emotional and imagistic level. As the main thread of the narrative is resumed, we realize that the solo, far from stopping the narrative, has also contributed to the atmosphere of the play, and thus works on a dramatic level. As the play moves along easily, its improvisatory cadences contain ever-quickening impulses that gather force toward a cataclysmic ending, like a shattering crescendo.

Personal reminiscences and storytelling—with their natural propensity toward dramatic expression, and in keeping with the black tradition of the spoken word as the vehicle to transmit common values and history—are integral features of Wilson's plays. In *Fences,* for example, the characters sit around a porch engaged in daily rituals of joking, storytelling, and arguing; and, as in all the plays, the plot subtly inches forward toward a final confrontation.

Storytelling, as a form of black expression, derives from an African tradition continued in slave tales, particularly trickster tales, which reflected the same cultural metaphors attested to and preserved by slave songs and spirituals. According to Lawrence Levine, "the slaves' ready identification with animals in their tales revealed . . . a tendency to see themselves as part of a unified world in which Man, beasts, spirits, even inanimate objects, were a natural part of the order of things. . . . Slave tales no less than slave songs or folk beliefs were fashioned within this world view and derived much of their substance and meaning from it" (133). The tales were an integral part of the same folk continuum authenticated by the music, and their impact on black life was complex and varied (Levine 115). They were not just "clever tales of wish-fulfillment through which slaves could escape from the imperatives of their world . . . [but were also] painfully realistic stories which taught the art of surviving and even triumphing in the face of a hostile environment" (Levine 115). Essentially an artistic distillation of a cultural memory, they afforded blacks an opportunity to witness and comprehend their present affliction. Like the blues, the tales were an affirmation, for better or worse, of personal and collective experience. Like the blues, therefore, the performance of the story was as important as the words themselves; indeed, the performance was often the narrative itself.

The breaks, slides, and percussive effects used by a blues guitarist to create complex, polyrhythmic patterns, and the reechoing of this sliding technique in the singing of the blues—with its guttural sounds, stretched syllables, and inserted pauses—are as important to the emotional content of a blues performance as the semantics of the lyrics themselves. A "downhome" blues singer's words are often slurred or trailed off, with the music continuing the line, thus underscoring the equal importance of the instrumental and vocal parts to the melody. This kind of embellishment characteristic of a blues performance is also intrinsic to the raconteur's art. Levine describes it:

Slave versions of history, like all slave tales, were enhanced by the manner of their delivery. The oral inventiveness of good storytellers . . . was a source of delight and stimulation to their audiences. Their narratives were interlarded with chants, mimicry, rhymes, and songs. . . . Nothing, it seems, was too difficult for a storyteller to represent: the chanting sermon of a black preacher and the response of his entire congregation, the sounds of a railway engine, the cries

of barnyard animals, the eerie moans of spectral beings, all formed
an integral part of black tales. (88–89)

Storytelling is therefore essential to the form and substance of much
black drama, for in it are theatrically codified the experiences and
cultural impulses of black Americans. With the blues, it takes its place
on the "panoply of expressive strategies that serves as a unifying
principle for black identity" (Harrison 294). Wilson uses both these
strategies in the underlying structure, thematic content, and development of his plays.

In the following pages, I will analyze in detail each of the four plays
included in this study to show how Wilson uses these recurrent patterns, themes, and strategies to portray the lives of his characters and
to chronicle their odysseys toward reunion, wholeness, and self-
authentication.

1

MA RAINEY'S BLACK BOTTOM

A COLLISION OF BLUES AND SWING

Throughout the twentieth century black music has been in a continuous state of evolution, with a new mode of expression marking virtually every decade. There were the additive rhythms of ragtime; the twelve-bar call and response of the blues; jazz, swing, and the big band; be-bop and dazzling virtuosity; and fusion and the marriage of acoustic and electronic instruments. And, just when it seemed that the only possibilities were a reworking of old styles, rap emerged with its hard, driving rhythms, staccato vocals that simulated electronic voices, dance movements at once fluid and robotic, and lyrics that recalled the blues in their cries of protest.

In 1927, black music took one of these major leaps. The Harlem Renaissance was in its tenth year, and black musicians were gaining wide popularity after King Oliver's historic recording session four years earlier in 1923.[1] In this same year, Duke Ellington launched his legendary Cotton Club engagement in Harlem, Count Basie embarked on his Kansas City career,[2] and Louis Armstrong emerged from the shadow of Oliver's band with his "Hot Five" and "Hot Seven" recordings. Jazz was poised on the threshold of a new sound and a new era—swing and the big band.

It is in this changing era that Wilson sets his play *Ma Rainey's Black Bottom*, which takes place in a studio in Chicago in 1927 during a recording session by the blues singer Ma Rainey and her four black musician sidemen. The significance of this date echoes strongly through the play, for much of the action flows from a conflict between proponents of the old and new forms of black music: between the blues and swing.

Wilson clearly sketches this division early in the play through the stage directions accompanying the entrances of the characters. He draws a sharp distinction between the three older sidemen—Cutler, Toledo, and Slow Drag—and the younger Levee. Cutler, the trombonist and guitar player, is the "most sensible," with a playing style that is "solid and almost totally unembellished"; Toledo, the pianist, "recognizes that [his instrument's] limitations are an extension of himself" and "his insights are thought-provoking"; and Slow Drag, the bassist, is "deceptively intelligent, though, as his name implies, he appears to be slow." Levee is more flamboyant and "somewhat of a buffoon," with a "rakish and bright" temper and strident voice. Their personalities also reflect their attitudes toward music: the older three favor the more plaintive, deeply emotional sounds of the blues; Levee, the flashier rhythms of swing.

As he unfolds the events in the play and reveals the characters' stories of their past experiences, Wilson affords us glimpses into the development of their personalities and allows us to be privy to their efforts to survive the social and economic injustices that beset blacks in the early part of the twentieth century. Since music is an integral part of the lives and racial identity of these characters, much of the conflict centers around their music. The clash of the characters' personalities reflects the struggle for self-affirmation that blacks faced in the late 1920s.

From the beginning of the play Levee is the isolated figure, set apart from his fellow musicians by his youth and arrogance. Like the sound of his trumpet, his brashness rises stridently above the muted personalities of his older colleagues, the impatient notes and words clashing discordantly against the unembellished rhythms of the others. Determined to start his own band, his ambition is fueled by Sturdyvant, the white producer who promised a recording contract for his songs, songs written in Levee's version of the emerging swing style.

"Something wild . . . with a lot of rhythm," as Sturdyvant puts it. Levee has no patience with the old style, dismissing it as rudimentary, and he is unwilling to rehearse their accompaniment of Ma Rainey's blues. This dissension between him and the others, later including Ma Rainey, is the basis for much of the dramatic conflict of the play. Bolstered by his ability to write music and brashly confident in his talent, he belittles the music they have gathered to play: "I knows how to play *real* music . . . not this old jug-band shit. I got style." To this Toledo replies, "Everybody got style. Style ain't nothing but keeping the same idea from beginning to end. Everybody got it."

To Toledo, style is indistinguishable from content; it is manifested in the artist's fidelity to the main musical idea or theme, whatever his improvisations. To Levee, who needs to put on his new shoes to "play some good music now," style is synonymous with attitude. To play well, he must look good. The connection between his shiny Florsheims and his music is a symbolic link that acquires an explosive dimension at the end of the play, when Sturdyvant's rejection of his songs is immediately followed by Toledo stepping on his shoes—the final straw that snaps Levee's control, precipitating the murder.

But there is a mythical dimension to Levee's behavior. Harrison's suggestion that Levee owes his pedigree to the Yoruba trickster deity Eshu (309) lifts him from the purely social sphere of the itinerant musician and locates him and his behavior in a cultural realm integral to the development of the African-American ethos. Divine tricksters abound in the mythological traditions of most cultures, whether it be the Hindu Krishna teasing the *gopis* (milkmaids), the phallic Greek god Hermes and his thieving son, Autolycus, or such mischievous African mythic figures as the Dahomean Legba or the Yoruban Eshu. In their seeming lawlessness, they represent the rebellious energy that inveighs against norms and strictures, the roaming spirit of creativity and procreativity that dances to its own rhythms in a cocky and arrogant celebration of individual will. In her essay "Feminity in Yoruba Art," Clara Odugbesan discusses this aspect and writes that Eshu is "associated with disorderliness and confusion. . . . he is the equivalent of the 'tempter' rather than the 'devil' in Christian ideas" (201).

From this destructiveness arises true creativity, the pioneering chutzpah that will not be contained within neat parameters of accepted behavior but bursts forth in a wild explosion as ancient and enduring as a Dionysian revel or a mardi gras pageant. It is the spirit that roves the outskirts of society, the artistic steppenwolf in quest of self-authentication, seeking ways to reshape its destiny. In African-American folklore, this energy found expression in the animal trickster tales of the slaves. The trickster occupied a central position in their consciousness, for his pranks represented the victory of the weak over the strong. This depiction of the victorious weak, however, existed only at the most elemental level. Mere survival was not all the trickster wanted. He had his eyes set on most of the goals that human beings seek—wealth, power, glory, sexual gratification. But, as Levine writes, his exploits were not always romanticized. "The universe held promise and hope, but it was also dominated by malevolence, injustice, arbitrary judgement, and paradox which had to be dealt with here and now. . . . At no point did slaves allow romanticism to dilute their vision of the world. The trickster was often celebrated, to be sure, since in his victories slaves could experience vicarious joy. But he was portrayed in hard and realistic terms" (134).

In the persona of the trickster, black slaves found a continuing way to reappraise their situation, to renegotiate their fluctuating relationship with their world and their masters. It is in this persona that Levee finds the freedom, "like a pesty boll weevil with an indiscriminating appetite, [to set] his sights on a feast in the midst of moral and spiritual famine" (Harrison 308). Unfortunately, his incontinent spirit is allowed no room to overflow. Trapped by social hatred and discrimination, and out of step with the times, he is alienated from everyone around him, including himself. The trickster, bent on survival and secure in a sense of indestructability, very easily slips into actions that are destructive to himself and to his community.

Levee's disparaging attitude toward the blues reflects his mythological heritage, for "the one central feature of almost all trickster tales is their assault upon deeply ingrained and culturally sanctioned values" (Levine 104). Any doctrines that demand fealty are antithetical to the very nature of the self-empowered trickster, who finds such coercive stipulations discordant with the inner rhythms urging him along an unrestricted individual path. This arrogance, motivated by the instinct for survival, can sometimes blind the trickster to the deeper truths in the values he debunks. Levee fails to see that swing is not a denial of but a natural evolution from the older form of music. Each new form is built upon older forms in such a manner that the earlier forms are often recognizable. This is particularly true of the blues, which, because of its distinct structure, is transparent in most forms that use it; and every new mode of jazz, including swing, incorporated the blues.[3] But Levee's musicianship is not yet mature enough to perceive the understructure of blues in this new form that has caught his fancy.

Most of the great jazz artists viewed themselves as torchbearers rather than inventors. Louis Armstrong, Duke Ellington, Count Basie, Charlie Parker, and others were great innovators who were acutely aware of carrying on a tradition. This has as much to do with the nature of black life as with the character of the music. The oral tradition is an integral part of the lives of black Americans, a legacy from their African roots when the history and myths of a tribe were kept alive by *griots*.[4] Wherever the bardic tradition thrived—ancient Greece, Africa, India, and other parts of Asia—the performance of the singer/poet was no mere narrative but an artistic rendition in a communal setting that revitalized culturally sanctioned myths. Storytelling and the performance of the blues—particularly in its improvisatory aspect—are part of this tradition in which cultural values and codes are transmitted from generation to generation, and where older performers are looked upon as gurus from whom the younger aspirants may learn and then forge their own artistic destinies.

But Levee's impatience leads him to ignore this sense of tradition. His swing arrangement of "Ma Rainey's Black Bottom" focuses more on a jaunty orchestration of the piece—with Toledo's piano and Slow Drag's bass providing the rhythm, and the winds (Cutler's trombone and Levee's own trumpet) improvising on the breaks—than on providing the best backing for Ma Rainey. His individual streak rebels against the fact that this band, as Cutler says, "ain't none of them hot bands. [It] is an accompaniment band." Levee is not content with being an accompanist. He does not care that the song is actually a vehicle for Ma Rainey, for he is more concerned with swinging the tune ("Now we gonna dance it . . . but we ain't gonna countrify it") than with backing the singer. "Ma come in over the top. She got to find her own way in."

Levee suffers from an almost classic case of hubris, for his outrageous behavior is the result of a defiance of tradition as he pursues his own destiny.[5] It is his pride that generates his indifferent attitude toward Ma and her music at the beginning of the play. By shunning the blues, he turns his back on the most important aspect of his musical heritage. It is also a denial of an essential part of his identity as a black American, a part woven into the fabric of all the traditions that inform his sensibilities. In seeking to discover his own identity through the new music, he chooses to reject the old music that defines the identity of his race. More ironic is the fact that in his desperation to win a recording contract he seeks approval and artistic direction from Sturdyvant, the white record producer. The result is a hodgepodge of new rhythms and changes made to suit a businessman who has no artistic feel for the music.

By ingratiating himself with Sturdyvant, Levee becomes virtually an apostate to his fellow musicians, aligning himself with the white man and bestowing on him the authority to make decisions about the one thing that is truly their own—their music. Toledo's comments are insightful: "As long as the colored man look to white folks to put the crown on what he say . . . as long as he looks to white folks for approval . . . then he ain't never gonna find out who he is and what he's about. He's just gonna be about what white folks want him to be about" (37). Levee faces the eternal dilemma of minorities, where success often is dependent on the approval of the majority. When that majority is also the oppressor, any attempt to pander to it is viewed as "selling out." To get his records produced, Levee feels he has to woo Sturdyvant. When the producer looks in on them, he jumps up, eager to please, with shuffling feet and ingratiating tone, prompting Cutler to say mockingly, "You hear Levee? You hear this nigger? 'Yessuh, we's rehearsing, boss.'"

But Levee does not consider his behavior sycophantic. From his father he has learned to deal with the white man, to smile in his face, shake his hand, look him in the eye, and bide his time: "I seen my daddy go up and grin in this cracker's face . . . smile in his face and sell him his land. All the while he's planning how he's gonna get him and what he's gonna do to him. That taught me how to handle them. So you all just back up and leave Levee alone about the white man. I can smile and say yessir to whoever I please. I got time coming to me. You all just leave Levee alone about the white man" (70). This is the language of the trickster, a philosophy fashioned from a need to survive and prevail. His eyes set on the ultimate goal of getting his songs produced, Levee will swallow his pride and mouth the words—and they are only words, after all—that Sturdyvant wants to hear. Like his wily mythological ancestor Brer Rabbit, Levee has no qualms about using any means necessary to outwit his stronger opponent and attain his ends. The trickster tales that sanction Levee's behavior were unequivocal in their objectives, as Levine has outlined them. "They encouraged trickery and guile; they stimulated the search for ways out of the system; they inbred a contempt for the powerful and an admiration for the perseverance and even the wisdom of the undermen; they constituted an intragroup lore which must have intensified feelings of distance from the world of the slaveholder" (132–33).

His father's death and the persistent memory of his mother's rape have imbued Levee with a deep desire for revenge, and he regards his musical talent as a weapon to get even with the white man. The world owes him a debt, and he is determined to take it. He wants redress and the respectability his parents never had. Although he rejects Ma's style of singing, he admires the way she wields her power over the white man. He does not realize that Ma's power comes from being true to herself and her music. She does not pander to Sturdyvant or Irvin and the changes they seek to make in her music. Having been on the road for several years and with so many records behind her, she knows her audiences and what they want. Refusing to compromise her music, she proves that success does not always depend on the approval of the majority. It does, however, depend on knowing the white men who do business with her; and she has no illusions about their motives: "Wanna take my voice and trap it in them fancy boxes with all them buttons and dials. . . . They don't care nothing about me. All they want is my voice. . . . As soon as they get my voice down on them recording machines, then it's just like if I'd be some whore and they roll over and put their pants on. . . . If you colored and can make them some money, then you all right with them. Otherwise, you just a dog in the alley" (79).

It is this complete knowledge of the people with whom she deals that makes Ma successful. But she has paid a high price for it. Her words reflect the bitterness of a woman who has had to struggle against a hostile society that gave her nothing and sought to grab all she had. We sense clearly the agonies and frustrations of this supremely talented woman forced to place her genius in the hands of a bunch of crude businessmen. In her terse tones linger the echoes of a long, tiring journey to her present position of power, obtained despite the odds, and because she never lost sight of whence she came.

Ma does not forget these roots. She gives her nephew Sylvester a job and a chance to perform with dignity. Though she is brusque and curt with Irvin and Sturdyvant, Ma displays an infinite patience with the stammering Sylvester, lovingly nursing him past his disability and drawing from him a clean performance when it seemed certain to everyone that he was beyond hope. The result is a testimony to the fact that, with nurturing, anyone can perform with credit.

It is significant that a nonmusician plays an important role in the recording. The inarticulate Sylvester represents those black people with little or no voice in this society. By letting him do the introduction, Ma Rainey suggests that they too can participate in the blues—all blacks have a voice through their music—and, in a larger sense, that they can contribute to the successful advancement of black culture. Levee's vociferous opposition to Sylvester's role highlights the contrast between them—Sylvester's few words are used to promote his heritage, the blues; Levee's verbiage debunks and denies that heritage. The results are noteworthy—Sylvester is triumphant (he manages to do the introduction without a mistake); Levee ultimately is destroyed. One lesson from the trickster tradition is that loquaciousness leads to trouble. Keeping one's mouth shut was one of the morals of the trickster tales. "The concluding lines of these widely told stories repeated one message over and over: It's bad to talk too much. I told you something that got me here would get you here. You talk too much. I told you tongue brought me here and tongue is what brought you here" (Levine 99).

Another part of Ma's roots, perhaps the most significant part, is the blues. Resisting any attempt to "swing" the blues, she sings it the way she has always sung it, the way she believes it was meant to be sung. Her strength comes from a deep understanding of the sensibilities that inform the blues. Any attempt to tamper with it is tantamount to a personal attack on her; to compromise this music is to desecrate the thing most sacred to her, the essence of her identity. The mere suggestion to revise her song incurs her wrath, and from the moment she hears about Levee's rearrangement his days with her band are numbered. His swing interpretations, which incorporate Sturdyvant's suggestions, are in direct conflict with her blues, and his claim that improvisation is the key to the music angers her further. Refusing to accept his function as an accompanist for Ma and fired up by Sturdyvant's promises, he takes her on and is dismissed.

But if improvisation is the essence of jazz, should Levee be denied the freedom to play his own style of music? After all, he only wants to add to a tradition that evolved from the improvisations that others—including Ma Rainey—had the freedom to make. Unfortunately, in his hurry to "arrive" he forgets the first principle of jazz—a debt to the past. The right to improvise bears with it the responsibility of being faithful to all the conventions that make jazz improvisation a great art—not just the spontaneous emotional response of the artist/performer to the music, but also the manner in which improvisers study and build upon earlier styles, "[leaning] heavily, in the creative sense, on all the music they've ever heard" (Coker 77). But Levee cares little for tradition. The present and future, in particular the fame and power they offer, obscure the past. He is more concerned with making records than with playing the music; content to rely on his talent, he is unwilling to perfect his skill.

Levee's ambition has stunted his musical growth. Although his attitude obviously springs from a desire to control his life and destiny, it grows so obsessive that it forces him into actions that isolate him from the only people who can help him discover himself as a musician and a person. He eschews his own people because he does not recognize them for the real friends they can be and turns instead to the white man as he seeks to fulfill his destiny through a contract with a member of the same race that destroyed his family and cast him adrift in the first place. Against his intuition, he places his trust in this record producer who, by his own admission, would rather be in the textile business. In the end, Sturdyvant rejects Levee despite his insistence that only he can play his songs. Such a claim is patently false. Having severed himself from the roots of his music, it is not truly his own; he is not essential to its performance, and it is easily taken away from him for a paltry five dollars per song. By taking Sturdyvant's advice on how to play his music, he betrays his deepest roots and himself. Spiritual rupture usually leads to self-destruction, and the devastated Levee turns against his own people and, in a very real sense, against himself.

Levee's behavior would be inconceivable to Ma because she is inseparable from her music, and no one can take it away from her. Although she is called the Mother of the Blues, she is the first to admit that she did not create the blues. ("I ain't started the blues way of singing . . . the blues always been there.")[6] She sees herself merely as a vehicle for it, a messenger who has helped bring the healing power of this music to the world. A mother is not, strictly speaking, a creator of Life but one who brings a manifestation of Life into the world, nurturing and encouraging it to grow. This title seems to suit Ma Rainey's role as a blues singer. Her simple humility in refusing to place the artist above the art contrasts sharply with Levee's cocky attitude when asked how he came to learn to write music: "I just picked it up . . . like you pick up anything. . . . But everybody can't play like I do." Instead of the suffering artist, there is in Levee's glibness a lack of reverence for the music. This arrogance is tested a minute later through a symbolic challenge when he claims he can spell *music* and then gets it wrong. Here is a confused, immature youth struggling to find his true identity, unsure of the precise nature of his role either as a black musician among other black musicians or as a black man in a white world.

It is significant that Levee plays the trumpet, the most flamboyant instrument in a jazz band. Capable of producing brilliant notes in the hands of such masters as Louis Armstrong, Miles Davis, and Dizzie Gillespie, the trumpet is in many ways the ideal instrument for the "rakish and bright" Levee. But he is not yet as good as he thinks he is. Wilson's description of his musicianship is quite revealing: "His voice is strident and totally dependent on his manipulation of breath. He plays wrong notes frequently. He often gets his skill and talent confused with each other" (23). He has the talent to be a good trumpet player but is still in the process of discovering his instrument, a process symbolically linked to self-discovery. Unlike his fellow musicians, he knows how to write music and therefore has the potential to be a composer and arranger. In the true tradition of a jazz musician, he sees himself as an improviser, even a virtuoso player. But unless he can acknowledge his debt to the past, he may never truly understand the art of improvisation.

By disavowing the roots of his music, Levee repudiates its very form and substance, for it has been created from the experience of all black Americans. Flavored with the smells and sounds of the "narrow crooked streets of East St. Louis, or the streets of [Chicago's] Southside," with roots in Alabama and Mississippi, it is a music replete with "warmth and redress . . . braggadocio and roughly poignant comments . . . vision and prayer" (Introduction). Compressed into its swells and full blown sounds are the agony and passion of several generations and a million lifetimes of slavery. And somewhere in the folds of its vibrant texture is the echo of every single tragedy that informed it, including Levee's personal grief. Until he fully appreciates this, he is doomed to prostitute his musical heritage to curry favor with boorish businessmen like Sturdyvant and to deceive himself into thinking he can be a star without honing his skill to match his talent.

Levee's talent is acknowledged by Cutler: "Levee's all right. He plays good music when he puts his mind to it." But staying focused is difficult for Levee, whose spirit smarts from the welts of his terrible childhood experiences, the memories of which have shaped his personality and his response to the world around him: "Life ain't shit.

You can put it in a paper bag and carry it around with you. It ain't got no balls. Now, death . . . death got some style! Death will kick your ass and make you wish you had never been born! That's how bad death is! But you can rule over life. Life ain't nothing" (92). This is the vision of a man who has felt the deepest despair, with firsthand knowledge of life without meaning. We are told only about one tragic experience—his mother's rape followed by his father's lynching. We can only guess at the rest of his life. Into it Wilson has distilled the essence of a thousand other desperate lives—sons and daughters of black slaves who grew up legally free but practically enslaved by a system that regarded them as less than human, objects to be used and abused. We do not know all the particulars of this life, but the pattern is familiar: years of poverty without a father or a proper home, living with a mother who had to deal with the harrowing experience of gang-rape. At some point in this appalling existence music probably offered a solution, and Levee took it. The trumpet was his way out of the slum, his ticket to the big city. Without it he would still be down there, grubbing for a meager existence. Toledo reproves him for being ungrateful that he is not performing the menial tasks usually given to black people. But that, to Levee, is the path of passivity. He will not be satisfied with tidbits. He wants it all. Like his guiding spirit, Brer Rabbit, he is not content with mere survival. The problem is that he does not know what he really wants. Having lived so long in despair, he is incapable of shaping any definable goal for himself, and he finds meaning only in death. The manner of his father's death was glorious, something to learn from and emulate. Life is pale and empty, death has style; and style, to Levee, is everything. In his fascination with death, he unconsciously denies himself any chance at life. Embittered by the raw deal society has given him, he plunges into self-destruction.

According to Toledo, the journey to complete emancipation, to the "whole hog," will begin when black people fully understand that self-help is their only real option, for the white man will always regard them as unwanted leftovers. Toledo is talking about true self-knowledge—the ability to accept the facts about one's position in society at large, no matter how unseemly or unflattering, and then to seek self-affirmation within one's own cultural community. However justified Levee's dissatisfaction might be, his success depends on the musical traditions of his own people, not on Sturdyvant. Ma understands this fully. She knows that her commercial success is the result of an artistic connection with her cultural roots. On a lesser scale, the other musicians have varying degrees of this self-knowledge. They also know their limitations and have a strong sense of their roles as musicians. Aware that no white man will give them a handout, they depend on Ma, their musical heritage, and their own talents for their fulfillment as musicians. Content with being her sidemen, they are very successful in those roles and better able to negotiate their way in a white society.

Lacking this perspective, Levee is a poor judge of people. Full of bitterness and arrogance, he is vulnerable to exploitation. Sturdyvant proves this, and even Dussie Mae is ready to take advantage of him. Before she enters, Slow Drag describes her opportunistic ways. ("She told Levee he'd have to turn his money green before he could talk to her"). When we meet her it is obvious that her interest in Levee peaks only after she discovers he really can write music and might well get his own band. She makes no bones about the fact that her favors will be traded only for something tangible—when he gets his band she will be available. Her promises add a splash of color to Levee's image of himself—a powerful, popular musician with his own songs and his own girl. But nobody really wants him—Sturdyvant wants his songs, and Dussie Mae wants the trappings of his success.

But Dussie Mae, like Levee, is desperately trying to survive on her own. Without the talent and enterprise of a Ma Rainey, she needs to ensure her own security in any relationship, for it is obvious that Levee's interest in her is only sexual: "A man what's gonna get his own band need to have a woman like you. . . . I just wanna show you I know what the women like. They don't call me Sweet Lemonade for nothing. . . . can I introduce my red rooster to your brown hen? . . . Now I know why my grandpappy sat on the back porch with his straight razor when grandma hung out the wash. . . . I bet you sound like the midnight train from Alabama when it crosses the Mason-Dixon line" (81–82). This is the voluptuous dance of the phallocentric trickster seeking self-authentication in a triumphant acknowledgment of his procreative fecundity. It is an unconscious tribute to his ancestor, the Yoruban Eshu, god of procreativity, endowed with "long phallic hairdressing" (Odugbesan 204). The deeper level of Levee's relationship with Dussie Mae finds two lost souls yearning for some contact with each other in a society that would deny them the opportunity to flourish to the full extent of their potential. Desperate and dispirited, Dussie Mae will welcome any moment of human contact to fill some of the spaces in her vacuous existence. Despite her bravado, she finally capitulates, unable to resist Levee's advances.

Dussie Mae's character is not explicitly defined. Cutler refers to her as "Ma's gal" and tries to warn Levee to stay away from her. She is obviously Ma's lover, and the two of them make an interesting study in contrast. Ma is confident, sharp, and knows exactly who she is and what she wants; her music and talent serve as a bulwark against a hostile society. Dussie Mae seems lost and out of her depth in this world of male musicians, longing for a meaningful relationship, with little to offer except her sexuality. With no identity of her own and dependent on Ma for everything, she is like a doll on display, dressed up "to look nice for [Ma]." In their desperation to find companionship, Dussie Mae and Levee make a fatal error. They "betray" Ma and give her further cause to get rid of Levee.

Ma's confidence and security provide a protective mantle for Toledo, Slow Drag, and Cutler. With no pretensions about their musical abilities or aspirations to anything beyond their present status as Ma's sidemen, they appear to have settled into a comfortable niche. This in no way implies a lethargy or lack of enterprise. They are the sidemen of one of the greatest blues singers of their time, jobs that give them steady work and the opportunity to make a living doing something they love. Slow Drag is the most tolerant character, content to play his music, always seeking to avoid confrontation. When the others argue with Levee about the way to play Ma's song, he is just anxious to start practicing the songs so they can "get it right the first time and get it over with." He refuses to get involved in the argument over which version to play: "Don't make no difference. Long as we get paid." A thorough professional, he is ready and willing to play whatever is asked of him, as long as he can rehearse it first. When Sylvester stutters through his lines, Slow Drag suggests they "rehearse so the boy can get it right."

The bassist is the heartbeat of a jazz band. He lays down the pulse, anchoring the incessant rhythm from which the riffs and flights of the other instruments can take wing. Slow Drag embodies some of the solid characteristics of his instrument. Throughout the play, he manages to stay calm and unaffected by the events around him. Although, like his name, he appears somewhat slow, even a bit phlegmatic, there is a reassuring quality to his homespun philosophy. His reply to Toledo's criticism of black people demonstrates a dogged faith in the ability of his race to survive: "Well, the colored man's gonna be all right. He got through slavery, and he'll get through whatever else the white man put on him. I ain't worried about that. Good times is what makes life worth living. Now you take the white man. . . . The white man don't know how to have a good time. That's why he's troubled all the time. He don't know how to laugh at life" (41). Like the steady line of his bass, there is something enduring in Slow Drag's attitude toward life. He refuses to let problems affect him unduly, concentrating his energies on surviving. He believes in having a good time; in playing his music, drinking his liquor, smoking reefers, and leaving well enough alone, confident in his ability to get through any situation. The story of how he earned his nickname by finessing an enraged boyfriend into letting him slow dance with his girlfriend and the charming manner in which he talks Cutler out of a reefer reveal a cool audacity behind his laconic exterior. This hidden smoothness and ability to surprise are evident in his playing. As Wilson describes it: "Innate African rhythms underlie everything he plays, and he plays with an ease that is at times startling" (20).

Cutler, the guitarist and trombonist, is Slow Drag's kindred spirit. They have been together on the road for twenty-two years, and this bond is a source of strength and comfort to them. In the early days of jazz, before the swing era, the guitar had a limited role in a band, although it was an integral part of a blues soloist's performance. In a band of this kind the guitar was restricted to strumming and pulse-keeping, a companion role to that of the bass. The trombone's role was not much different—to keep time and rhythm as well as to provide some tonal depth and color. Reflecting his instrument's role, Cutler keeps the situation in the studio on an even keel. He is the leader of the group by virtue of his long association with Ma. He draws strength from the blues, his friendship with Ma, and his religious faith, and he is zealously protective of all three. That Levee attacks all three is evidence of the widening gulf between them. For a while, Cutler handles Levee's tantrums with great equanimity, even attempting to deflect Ma's anger away from the younger musician. But Levee's blasphemous attack on Christianity is too much even for Cutler to stomach, and he punches him in the mouth.

Like the guitar, the piano has occupied a central role in the development of black music, from the ragtime compositions of Scott Joplin and Eubie Blake to the barrelhouse blues of Jelly Roll Morton, the boogie-woogie style of James P. Johnson, the wit of Fats Waller, and the virtuosity of Art Tatum. While its individual contribution was enormous, particularly in the hands of the great musicians, its specific function in the rhythm section of a back-up band like this one was to supply the chord progression (this could be done by either the piano or the guitar).[7] Toledo's role, therefore, does not call for great virtuosity or individual innovation but is similar to the others in providing solid, if creative, rhythm backing for Ma's vocals. He "understands and recognizes that [his piano's] limitations are an extension of himself" and is content to play his part to the best of his ability: "That's what you supposed to do, ain't it? Play the music. Ain't nothing abstract about it." His no-nonsense demeanor is irritated by Levee's pretentious behavior, for he does not have Cutler's patience and will not suffer the younger man gladly. Throughout the play, they are at each other's throats. Having taught himself to read, Toledo is proud of his knowledge and tends to be rather scornful of Levee's brash immaturity: "Levee, you worse than ignorant, you ignorant without a premise" is his unlikely assessment of the young trumpeter. To him, the younger generation of blacks is too flippant about life and lacks a proper sense of direction.

Toledo's anger reflects a deep concern for the future of his race. When blacks were brought from different parts of Africa and "dropped into a pot like a stew," the expedience of slavery created a common destiny and a responsibility to shape their future in a liberating fashion. To fulfill this mission each of them must do something positive with his life. In Toledo's opinion, hard work is the way to forge the common identity that will save them from being swept away like so much offal. He sees Levee's frivolous attitude as a threat to that goal. But Slow Drag and Cutler challenge his insight:

SLOW DRAG: Toledo, just 'cause you like to read them books and study and whatnot . . . that's your good time. People get other things they likes to do to have a good time. Ain't no need you picking them about it.

CUTLER: Niggers been having a good time before you was born, and they gonna keep having a good time after you gone. (41)

Ralph Ellison's observation of the "near-tragic, near-comic lyricism" in the blues suggests an impulse that permits blacks to delve beneath the inhumane conditions of their lives and mine the layers of mirth nestling there. This ability to seize life and shake whatever joy they could out of the few moments that were given them is what saw them through decades of slavery and degradation. It is the springboard for the transcendent resolution of the spirituals and the hopeful resonance of the blues. Slow Drag and Cutler know that without this sense of joy they would be a people without luster; with it, they can survive the darkest night.

But for all the high spirits and easy camaraderie among this group of musicians, the ugly specter of racism continues to haunt them. Their sense of security within the studio fades like a phantom in the cold light of the forbidding city, where their identities dissolve into nameless, faceless black shadows floating about the fringes of the metropolis.[8] Ma's altercation with the cabby and the policeman is only a small example of the larger battles being fought in the streets. By allowing it to creep into the studio, Wilson suggests that her power, though considerable, is at best tenuous, confined only to the small pocket of the studio. Outside, she becomes just another target of white prejudice.

Throughout the play, the characters make several references to these battles in the world outside, forcing us to view the conflict within the studio—between Levee and the others—in the context of that world. Through their stories, we slowly begin to see these characters against a backdrop of racial hatred and discrimination. Their actions become the product of decades of social injustice, of prejudice that breeds the self-hate that finally ends in an explosion of black rage. These men and women—whose forefathers slaved to bring America to the twentieth century—are now dispensable commodities in a country hurrying to the top of the international ladder. Reflected in this small group of musicians is the story of a whole race of forgotten people, the "leftovers of history." They have served their purpose, and white America would like nothing better than to close its eyes and hope they just disappear. Honest, hard work fetches no rewards but creates suspicion and resentment instead—a well-earned check cannot be cashed except in a whorehouse, for it is only among society's dregs that blacks can expect recognition. Levee's father struggled to establish himself on his own land, only to have his white neighbors call him "an uppity nigger 'cause he done saved and borrowed to where he could buy this land and be independent." Then those same neighbors raped his wife and nearly killed his son, precipitating a course of events that led to vengeance and death.

No blacks are spared the ignominy of being scraps from history's table, whether they are successful singers like Ma Rainey or clergymen like Reverend Gates (in Cutler's story), who was humiliated by a crowd of white people in Sigsbee. The story prompts Levee to wonder why God did not save the decent clergyman and points to an interesting conflict embedded in the play, a conflict that Wilson deals with in greater detail in *Joe Turner's Come and Gone*—Christianity (the white man's religion) versus the African identity of blacks.

During their three hundred years of captivity, black people's link with their past was systematically corroded by laws and taboos imposed by white masters who sought increasing control over their slaves' minds and bodies. African rituals and customs were viewed as a threat and therefore forbidden,[9] for the more slaves were cut off from their roots the more malleable they would become. Chief among the white institutions that attempted to distance them from Africa was the Christian church. By forcing its God on blacks, the white church could control their spirits.[10] This process attempted, in part, to change the African into an imitation white man, a carbon copy of the European model; it was a process that robbed him of his individuality, dehumanized him, and turned him into chattel.

After emancipation, blacks discovered they had a nebulous social identity—they were neither slaves nor, in any real sense, free men and women. Rather, in one of the many strange effects of slavery, their social identity had been more defined before emancipation. Now, almost seventy years later in this so-called free society, they can hold on to nothing that will define them or reassure them that they are more than an aimless cluster of confused souls—nothing except their African roots. Denied full participation in the fellowship of America, cheated of their humanity by a dissembling social and legal system, their only hope of dispelling the angst that threatens to erode their lives resides in a renewal of spiritual ties with a distant past. This past has survived not only in their racial subconscious but, more tangibly, in their music, their stories, their almost ritualistic daily exchanges of banter configured along a call 'n' response pattern (Harrison 307) and their reinvented Christianity shot through with an African cosmology.

Toledo instinctively feels the weight of this process to change the black man. But his narrow vision sees only the end result of the transmogrification: "We done sold Africa for the price of tomatoes. We done sold ourselves to the white man in order to be like him. Look at the way you dressed. . . . That ain't African. That's the white man. We trying to be just like him. We done sold who we are in order to become someone else. We's imitation white men" (94). Cutler's response echoes centuries of helpless frustration, "What else we gonna be, living over here?" Sensing the futility of fighting a system that has dominated his race for over three hundred years, he is resigned to making the best of what he has. But Levee wants to fight back. He wants change in his life and music. He rejects all the institutions of the past, and the first to be discarded is Christianity: "He's a white man's God. . . . God ain't never listened to no nigger's prayers. God take a nigger's prayers and throw them in the garbage. God don't pay niggers no mind. In fact . . . God hate niggers! Hate them with all the fury in his heart. Jesus don't love you, nigger! Jesus hate your black ass! Come talking that shit to me. Talking about burning in hell! God can kiss my ass" (98).

Levee's image of Jesus as an oppressive white man is similar to Loomis's image (in *Joe Turner's Come and Gone*) of Jesus as a white overseer. Levee's hatred of Christianity is linked to his memory of his mother's rape, for he can still hear her cries of help:

> LEVEE: Cutler's God! Come on and save this nigger! Come on and save him like you did my mama! Save him like you did my mama! I heard her when she called you! I heard her when she said, "Lord, have mercy! Jesus, help me! Please, God, have mercy on me, Lord Jesus, help me!" And did you turn your back? Did you turn your back, Motherfucker? Did you turn your back? (99)

This leads to a scuffle with Cutler, a staunch Christian, and is followed by Levee's near-hysterical tirade against that same God, an invective-filled harangue toward heaven that ends with a scornful "your God ain't shit, Cutler." Unfortunately, unlike Loomis, Levee has no substitute for the God he rejects, for, along with all the other traditions, he has spurned any notion of his African heritage. In the first act, when they were discussing African customs, he had this to say: "I know he ain't talking about me. You don't see me running around in no jungle with no bone between my nose." The end of the play finds him cut off from his spiritual moorings, bereft of religion, tradition, and friends—with no recording contract, no job, and virtually no future.

Levee is not the only one who feels the repressive weight of Christianity—Toledo's marriage collapsed after his wife joined the church. Thus, the Christianity that separated Africans from their homeland continues to disrupt their homes, separating man from woman and husband from wife. It is no wonder that Eliza Cotter, the man in Slow Drag's story, sells his soul to the devil, the archenemy of Christianity. Once he has done that, he prospers beyond the expectations of any black man. Nor is it surprising that Mr. Cotter becomes an apostle for the devil, heading "north with that bag of his, handing out hundred-dollar bills on the spot to whoever wanted to sign on with the devil";[11] or that Levee would say, "That's the only thing I ask about the devil . . . to see him coming so I can sell him this [soul] I got. 'Cause if there's a god up there, he done went to sleep" (43).

Levee's antagonism toward Christianity is only one of his responses to racial prejudice. Most of the time, unfortunately, his tirades are directed against his own people—the result of rage and frustration brought on by years of injustice. In his interview with Bill Moyers, August Wilson said that the most valuable blacks were the ones in prison. They possess the warrior spirit that, in days of old, took men into danger in search of food for their families. Refusing to lie down and die, these men of destiny fought for what was denied them. Levee possesses this spirit.[12] Unwilling to settle for the white man's crumbs, he will fight for what he believes is his. For all his faults, he has the warrior spirit that launches him into a battle he may or may not win. But against such high odds his only option is to flail away wildly, and in the melee he cannot differentiate between friend and foe.

By giving his characters musical instruments to suit their personalities, Wilson creates a metaphor to explore the specific avenues that each of them has taken to find his identity as a black musician and a black American. The rhythm section of Cutler, Toledo, and Slow Drag walks a steady, balanced line between the commercially exploitative white world of Irvin and Sturdyvant and the abundant black world of Ma and the blues. They keep the former at bay by staying close and true to the latter, thus creating harmony out of potential dissonance. Levee, like his strident trumpet, constantly tries to break out on his own. He cannot be contained by either world and is in discord with both.

By setting *Ma Rainey* at the end of the 1920s, when black music was at a crossroad in its development, Wilson is able to explore one of the main roots of African-American culture and identity—the blues. Through a dramatic conflict between Ma Rainey, the blues singer, and Levee, a herald of the new emerging style of jazz—swing—Wilson suggests that black music—and particularly the blues—contains ancient cultural clues to the true identity of African Americans which they cannot ignore except at their peril. In his search for self-fulfillment and empowerment, Levee debunks his own traditions and turns to the white man for affirmation, thus ensuring his own destruction: when the white producer denies Levee the opportunity that he had promised, the young man kills one of his fellow musicians in frustration and rage, an act that slams the door on any hope of fulfilling his musical ambitions.

To tell the story of these musicians, Wilson uses the structure of a jazz piece. The characters engage one another in dialogue and banter and then, as on a break, each has a solo turn to talk about past experiences, which echoes another ancient African strategy of expression—storytelling. As point and counterpoint sharpen the dramatic conflict, and story riffs soar across the ensemble of conversation and action, the "music" of the play builds toward a shattering crescendo of murderous rage. At the end, we have a harrowing vision of the limited success and larger futility of trying to conquer attitudes hardened by centuries of social injustice; of frustrated attempts to be accepted as human beings; of cultural exploitation and the in-fighting that hopelessness breeds. Rising above the rubble of human debris is the triumphant blast of Levee's trumpet—redolent with the unconquerable, arrogant spirit of the trickster warrior.

2

FENCES

THE SINS OF THE FATHER...

While each of Wilson's plays reflects the political, social, and cultural mood of the decade in which it is set, the precise year of its setting has overtones that reverberate strongly through the piece. In *Ma Rainey's Black Bottom*, the year 1927—the threshold between the blues and swing eras—provided Wilson with a focal point for his dramatic action. *Fences* is set in 1957, exactly thirty years later. In that time several changes occurred in the social and cultural lives of black people.

By the fifties blacks were no longer a race of ex-slaves to be banished to the edge of town, although white America would have preferred them there. They were inching closer to the mainstream of American society. Reflected in their music were the complex changes this movement created in their identity as black Americans. Jazz, in different modes and styles, had dominated the musical scene of America for the past three decades, and a new movement was under way even as swing, big band, and blues artists like Louis Armstrong, Duke Ellington, Count Basie, and Eubie Blake continued to enjoy tremendous popularity. The early forties had seen the advent of bop, heralded and perfected by Charlie Parker, Dizzy Gillespie, and Thelonious Monk. In the late forties, rhythm 'n' blues came into its own, although it had been "evolving over a period of several years from the folk blues and other black-music styles" (Southern 499). By the late fifties, the old and new strands came together in the free jazz of John Coltrane and Charles Mingus. This whole period marked a new sophistication among jazz artists, with the emphasis on experimentation. Simple melodies were layered with complex harmonic structures as musicians stretched the rhythmic and dynamic boundaries of traditional jazz, seeking newer forms of expression.

The new sophistication evident in the music could also be seen in the way blacks renewed their struggles in the courts and streets of America. Having responded to their country's call for life and limb in the cause of the free world during World War II, they were ready to claim what had been denied them for so long—full citizenship. This was the decade in which they mounted their most spirited challenges on the bastions of white supremacy. In 1951, Thurgood Marshall launched the battle against desegregation that culminated in 1954, when Earl Warren's Supreme Court unanimously set aside Plessy v. Ferguson; in 1955, Rosa Parks ignited the civil rights movement and inspired a young Martin Luther King, Jr., to become its champion; and from 1957 to 1961,[1] in a series of legal battles, the U.S. judiciary consolidated the historic decision of 1954. In many ways, 1957 was one of the most important years of this decade, for in that year was enacted the first Civil Rights Act since the Reconstruction era, an act aimed at desegregating the franchise. This act also gave legal endorsement to blacks' right to protest discrimination. But it was only the very beginning. There was no telling how it would all turn out. The events of almost a century had underscored the distinction between de jure and de facto. Legally, blacks had been free for ninety-four years, but practically they had little or no access to any of the benefits that ordinary citizens take for granted—recourse to the law, equal employment opportunities, education. Thus, 1957 represented a time of some protest, much hope, and great skepticism—all of which are present in *Fences*.

This spirit of protest is manifested in the very first scene of the play when Troy Maxson, an ex-baseball player who works for a garbage collection company, tells his buddy, Bono, that he has protested to his bosses the unfairness of having black workers lift garbage while white workers drive the trucks. That a black garbage collector can do this without repercussion is a sign of the changing times. What is more significant is that he was told to "take it to the union." The winds of change had just started to blow. But, as Wilson writes in his introduction, they had "not yet begun to blow full."

The search for self-authentication in *Fences* is reflected in the attitudes and behavior of the characters within the social flux of the late fifties, in their individual and collective struggles to hew a niche for themselves in the rocky social terrain of postwar America. In *Ma Rainey,* Wilson uses a group of black musicians tucked away in a recording studio in Chicago as a microcosm to reflect the larger picture of blacks in urban America. In *Fences,* he focuses on the family, a blueprint to which he returns in *Joe Turner's Come and Gone* and *The Piano Lesson.* Over a period of eight years and through the use of narrative dialogue, Wilson traces the fortunes of the Maxson family for three generations. In their thwarted hopes and ambitions, their battered pride, their fears, their stubborn faith, their infidelities, and, ultimately, their survival, we glimpse the gargantuan efforts by a race of people who cling to the fringes of society and try to drag themselves into the mainstream to stand up and be counted.

Part of the play's action concentrates on Troy Maxson's refusal to accept the fact that social conditions are changing for the black man. This creates much of the dramatic conflict, leading to problems between him and his family, particularly his son Cory. Troy's obduracy springs from his bitterness over the fact that, despite his brilliant talent, he could not play major league baseball, while lesser white players became stars. He will not let Cory go to college on a football scholarship, arguing that there is no future in sports for the boy. His wife, Rose, reminds him that since Jackie Robinson's breakthrough, things are a little different now. But Troy will not be persuaded. Convinced of no professional future for black athletes, he is determined to direct his son into a more practical career.

Like Levee in *Ma Rainey,* Troy is a cultural descendant of Eshu. Imbued with a sense of indestructibility, he will not be denied entrance to the main banquet hall. Not for him the ancillary tables where the hired help grub for crumbs, where blacks are expected to be grateful for the half-opportunities thrown their way. If a hero is one who goes into a battle that he may or may not win, Troy Maxson possesses, in full measure, the same warrior spirit that fueled Levee's crusade. Like Levee, he wants complete satisfaction or nothing at all. The promise of change is empty; he cares only about change itself. Such an attitude is the prerogative of the self-empowered trickster whose goals are survival and success, whatever the consequences. The so-called realities of the social world around him matter little, for he dances to an internal rhythm, answering a call for self-authentication that springs from a cultural, even cosmological, dimension. Dissatisfied with the way things are, Troy pursues an individual riff that pulses far ahead of the phlegmatic rhythms of a slow-moving society. But, as with all tricksters, his actions are potentially destructive, and he finds himself estranged from the very family he is striving to protect. In the final analysis, however, we cannot judge him on a socially realistic level without considering also the mythological perspectives of his actions. In his magnificent struggle to nurture his family, he represents the purest strain of the survival instinct in the African-American race.

Separation is a major theme in this play, one that Wilson continues to explore in *Joe Turner's Come and Gone*. There are several references to people leaving their homes, families, and lovers. In many instances, the separation is linked to migration, where people take off down the road in search of new pastures. Bono's account of how his father left home represents a common pattern in black families during the early part of the twentieth century: "A lot of them did. Back in those days what you talking about.... they walk out their front door and just take on down one road or another and keep on walking.... Just keep on walking till you come to something else. Ain't you never heard of nobody having the walking blues? Well, that's what you call it when you just take off like that" (51). When the problems of sharecropping became too oppressive and the struggle to feed, clothe, and shelter a family under the despotic hand of white landlords grew intolerable, black folk just "upped and left." Staying would have destroyed their spirits. The price was high in terms of separation from one's family and loved ones, but even that was not something new, for slavery had inured them to the pain of familial disseverance.

In this play, separation takes a different form than it does in *Joe*

Turner, but in each play it leads to a search for fulfillment, for some kind of meaning in a futile existence. While separation is common in almost every society—where the young ones leave home to make their way in the world—it has a special significance among black Americans. Their separation, the result of a deep spiritual and social dislocation, was a desperate escape into hostile territory. The people Bono talks about were looking for a better life. They did not know what form or shape that life would take, or even if it existed; they knew only that, having reached the end of their tether in their present situation, they had to leave. Many had no idea where they were going; the important thing was that they were on the move. "The Walking Blues"[3]—a song that, in different versions, "musicians sang and played the length and breadth of the Mississippi Delta" (Palmer 4)—was the Delta Anthem. According to Muddy Waters, "that was the theme in Mississippi; most every guitar player played that" (Palmer 104).

Although Troy's father did not leave home despite being engulfed by a family of eleven children and a sharecropping system that left him little time for anything but work, his mother did run away, as did the other women in his father's life. Thus, very early Troy learned the agony of separation. But he also discovered that sometimes such an action was inevitable. When he was fourteen his father found him in a compromising position with a girl and beat him so severely that he decided to leave home. This was no act of spite but a rite of passage, one that followed his realization that he was no longer a boy but a man in the classic situation of being his father's competitor in that most primal of male conflicts—a fight over a female: "Now I thought he was mad 'cause I ain't done my work. But I see where he was chasing me off so he could have the gal for himself. When I see what the matter of it was, I lost all fear of my daddy. Right there is where I become a man . . . at fourteen years of age" (52).

With this perception, Troy donned the mantle of adulthood; he became his father's equal. Now he could slip from the yoke of the older man's domination and, by extension, from the dehumanizing effects of sharecropping. In separating himself from the farm, he was cutting loose the remaining bonds of slavery. Two stages of his emerging new identity were complete and both involved separation leading to freedom—from his father and from the farm. The next step was more difficult: empowerment as a free man in American society at large. He now had to deal with the psychological fetters of the past and the realities of life in a hostile social climate, as he searched for his true place in a community controlled by white men.

Often, separation from one's family is requisite to the search for self, and this need for detachment is evident in the actions of Troy's brother Gabriel. Even without full possession of his faculties Gabe has a fierce desire to be independent. Barely able to take care of himself, he feels that as long as he lives with Troy he will never realize his true potential as a free man. So he moves over to board with Miss Pearl, who gives him two rooms. Although Troy is upset over the move, Rose understands Gabe's longing to be independent, even though he was never really tied down. As Gabe holds up the key to his rooms his voice is filled with a triumphant glee: "That's my own key! Ain't nobody else got a key like that. That's my key! My two rooms!" To Gabe, freedom means the chance to live his own life the way he wants, and for now he is free. He is the Archangel Gabriel and the key in his hand opens the gates to his heaven on earth.

Troy discovered that leaving home was only the beginning of an uphill journey of survival. There were no guarantees. If anything, the struggle was more fierce. For many migrant blacks, slavery to white masters was replaced by slavery to poverty; square meals were traded for starvation; plantation shacks exchanged for riverbanks, sidewalks, and bridges; cotton fields yielded to alleys; overseers turned into policemen; the hot sun of the South gave way to the freezing wind of the North; and finally, the road to freedom ended in the penitentiary. But before landing in prison, Troy got married and had a son, Lyons. In an ironic circle, the act of separation that helped him break away from his old family led to separation from his new family.

Every act of separation marks a new stage in the development of one's identity. In prison, separated from his family, Troy found what he had been seeking—baseball. It gave him new direction, renewed meaning, and the opportunity to redefine himself and prove that he could do something well. It saved his life in prison and then became his raison d'être. Soon there was no distinction between Troy Maxson, human being, and Troy Maxson, baseball player.

After Troy left prison he played in the Negro baseball leagues, on a schedule so arduous only a passionate love for the game could make one endure it.[4] Like the blues musician, the black baseball player was forced into a nomadic existence, moving from town to town, playing almost every day from early spring to late fall. For blacks the only avenues to success and self-esteem, as well as freedom, involved a kind of rootlessness.

But black players, talented enough for the major leagues, were denied the opportunity to excel at the highest levels of the sport.[5] To Troy, this was tantamount to being denied a chance to grow. Having put all his energies into baseball, he longed for national recognition,[6] for this was America's game. This was where heroes were made, men who could hit a ball hard and long, or pitch with deadly accuracy, or catch a fly ball dropping out of the sky. Ted Williams said that baseball provided every American boy with a chance to excel (Peterson iii). Troy was never given that chance; at least, not in the best arenas in the country. Bono's praise that he ranks among the best players only draws a bitter cry from him: "What it ever get me? Ain't got a pot to piss in or a window to throw it out of." The game that was once a beacon in his life becomes a millstone round his neck, dragging him into the depths of acrimony, filling his life with bitterness, coloring all his attitudes, opinions, and relationships. He refuses to let Cory play football, for he considers his own life as an athlete a waste and wants to spare his son the same futility: "I don't want him to be like me! I want him as far away from my life as he can get. . . . I decided seventeen years ago that boy wasn't getting involved in no sports. Not after what they did to me in the sports" (39). In venting his anger on athletics, Troy is actually turning against himself. Like Levee, he attacks the source of his identity and, in seeking self-empowerment as a free human being, becomes a slave to bitterness. This, as we shall see, stunts the development of his full potential as a father, husband, and friend.

In Troy's experience, chance, or fate, has played an important role in directing his life. He believes that neither talent nor skill counts for much in America, where the color of one's skin becomes the decisive factor in the workplace, the playing field, or the street. Chance made him black, chance took him to Mobile when he was fourteen, chance led him into armed robbery, and chance brought him to baseball. Even Rose, realizing that only chance can improve their circumstances, tries her luck at gambling, although she is well aware that chance usually works against people like them: "Seems like those that need the least always get lucky."

To Troy, the idea of taking a chance on a lottery is foolish. Having been on the losing side of chance for so long, he knows it will never work for them. His optimism lies in a shattered heap, beside his unfulfilled dreams, on the baseball fields of black America. The only possible success left him—the only possible victory—is survival: enduring from dawn to dusk and day to day in a job that barely provides for his family. Were it not for the quirk of fate that injured Gabe and brought three thousand dollars in compensation, Troy might not have survived. When chance does work in his favor, the price is terrible: his brother's life is destroyed and he is haunted with guilt at having profited from that disaster. This guilt adds to his frustration at the soul-destroying struggle to make ends meet. Like his father before him, he is trapped in a maelstrom of hard labor.

In many ways, Troy's life comes full circle. He ran away from the farm and his father only to discover that escaping to the city could not exorcise his father's spirit. The realization that he is fated to be like his father increases his sense of helplessness, for he knows there is no eluding the drudgery of his destiny. He remembers his father having been in a similar trap, fighting to stay ahead of the sharecropping system. For the descendants of slaves, sharecropping was only a new kind of slavery—a variation on an old theme. And Troy's never-ending cycle of labor is merely a key modulation in that same concerto of grief.

Living such a life of drudgery is like living close to death, and that, indeed, is what happens to Troy. Every moment is a constant battle to survive, to stay alive. He says that during his bout with pneumonia he wrestled with Death, whom he describes as wearing a "white robe with a hood." Although the immediate symbolic reference is to the Ku Klux Klan, the symbol includes all white men as Death-like figures. But Troy has survived the pneumonia (his imaginary wrestling match), and from this experience he fashions a baseball metaphor to help him combat the doom that constantly threatens: "That's all death is to me. A fastball on the outside corner." Every batter needs a bit of luck to hit such a ball. The percentages are not favorable, however, when you are "born with two strikes on you before you come to the plate." But Troy's skill as a baseball player is matched by his skill as a survivor. He knows he cannot always keep that fastball from streaking past his swinging bat, but until it does he will play hard and survive as long as he can.

This is the pain Troy seeks to spare Cory, but, unable to avoid the parental trap, he dominates his son just as his own father had dominated him. By protecting Cory, Troy denies him the chance to pursue his own calling. Accusing Rose of "mothering that boy too much," he does exactly that himself. He says that Cory should make his own way without anyone holding his hand, yet he will not let the boy take a chance and try to survive as he himself did. Afraid that Cory will be destroyed by the same forces that hurt him, Troy clips his son's wings. But things are different now. When Troy was growing up, blacks were denied a proper high school education; today, they are being offered scholarships to college. Unfortunately, Troy is too consumed by acrimony to notice the great opportunity for Cory, whether or not he goes on to play professional football. In the fifties, athletics began to provide a second avenue—after music—for blacks to excel in ways that commanded the attention and admiration of white society. It is ironic that although Troy found self-esteem and pride through athletics, he would deny his son the same opportunity. In fact, he denies his son much more—the chance to get a college education and perhaps even to become a professional player.

Although Troy tries to protect his son, he is unable to show him any affection. Rose's suggestion that all Cory wants is his father's approval is met with a brusque "Rose I ain't got time for that." This is a hard man, the product of a severe school. With all his energies focused on survival, he has little time for parental affection. For him the greatest virtue is responsibility. The only time he praises his father is when he talks about the older man's sense of responsibility toward his children. When Cory, confused and hurt by his father's lack of affection, is constrained to ask why he does not like him, Troy responds with a speech about responsibility: he feeds, clothes, and shelters Cory, not because he likes him, but because it is his job, his responsibility.

This seeming lack of affection is hard on Cory, who obviously worships his father. But every attempt to emulate Troy is met with disapproval, and, slowly, their lives begin to revolve in concentric circles—beginning at the same center, destined to describe similar patterns, overlapping in some ways but without any real contact. As Troy cuts off every move Cory makes to follow in his footsteps as an athlete, the boy's frustration reaches a breaking point, and he attacks his father. Finally, the only moment of physical contact between them is one of violence and anger, just as it had been between Troy and his father. Then, paralleling the events of a generation ago, the son leaves home in search of his own identity. A new cycle has begun, launched by an act of physical and psychological separation. In attempting to steer Cory's life along a different path, Troy orchestrates exactly what he was trying to avoid. As Rose later tells Cory, "Your daddy wanted you to be everything he wasn't . . . and at the same time he tried to make you into everything he was."

But Cory makes a desperate bid to end the parallels. Believing he will discover himself only when he has dispelled his father's spirit, he joins the marines, a career as far removed from his father's as possible. But Cory cannot escape his father in the margins of society's professions, for Troy's true identity does not lie in the naturalized sphere of social roles; rather, it is in cosmic and mythological dimensions that his spirit acquires the authentication it seeks: like the trickster he emulates, he is a survivor, and many of his actions—particularly the ones that directly affect Cory—spring from his pursuit of a cultural destiny. Thus, wherever Cory goes, Troy's large shadow continues to hover over him. The more he tries to exorcise his father's spirit, the more tightly it grabs hold of him. On the day of Troy's funeral, Cory's anguish is evident as he refuses to go to the ceremony, grappling with his father's memory like a fragile butterfly struggling to break free of its cocoon:

CORY: I can't drag Papa with me everywhere I go. I've got to say no to him. One time in my life I've got to say no. (96)

But Cory is also wrestling with his own emerging identity, for, as Rose tells him, they are alike, father and son. She knows that Cory's refusal to attend the funeral will only increase his bitterness. She knows that by rejecting his father Cory is only rejecting himself. He has to find another way.

In the prelude to the play August Wilson writes:

> When the sins of our fathers visit us
> We do not have to play host.
> We can banish them with forgiveness
> As God, in His Largeness and Laws.

This is the only way for Cory. As long as he is separated from his father, he remains separated from his true self. The only course is reconciliation—a reunion between father and son; a recognition by Cory that it is left to him to accept the best of his father in him and banish the worst; to celebrate the strength of character that survived half a century of prejudice and forgive the pain that came out of that battle.

That Cory can accept his father's spirit in him—something Troy could not do—is as much a testament to the times in which he lives as it is to his character. He is not contained by the same circumstances that beset his father and grandfather, for he lives in the sixties, a decade of some hope for blacks.[7] His career in the marines is not an echo of the variations of slavery endured by his father and grandfather. Once he welcomes his father's spirit, he is free to sing his father's song. Troy's daughter, Raynell, joins him, and as they sing we can almost hear Troy's voice singing with them, for this is the song he used to sing, the song made up by his father. In the final scene of the play, three generations of Maxsons are reconciled; in this old song are harmonized the voices and spirits of two fathers and two sons—and the sins of the father are truly forgiven.

There is a marked difference in Troy's relationship with each of his two sons. Cory is relentlessly pursued and steered away from any involvement in sports. He must perform household chores and hold down a job at the A&P. Lyons, Troy's older son by a former marriage, is more hail-fellow-well-met. He does no work, lives off his wife's earnings—when she has a job—and every now and then comes to "borrow" money from his father, who criticizes his lazy lifestyle, exhorts him to get a job, but always ends by giving him the money. Perhaps Troy feels guilty because he was in prison when Lyons was a child. At one point, Lyons even reproaches his father for trying to change him now after having been absent during his formative years, thereby further compounding his father's guilt feelings.

Using his charm and geniality to get by, Lyons seems to float through this world without any real purpose. While Troy, motivated by a strong sense of responsibility, chooses to fight his way past a hostile system, Lyons chooses just the opposite. Faced with an oppressive society, he ignores it by refusing to get a job that would place him in a vulnerable position: "I don't wanna be carrying nobody's rubbish. I don't wanna be punching nobody's time clock." Troy is a garbage collector not because he likes it but because it is the only job available. The work is a means to an end; he dignifies it by taking pride in his ability to provide for his family. He is a survivor and the fruits of his toil are food on his table, clothes on his family, and a roof over their heads. Lyons, on the other hand, blithely unconcerned about his easygoing lifestyle, is content to while away his hours at a club. A bon vivant, he dresses stylishly and uses his special brand of bonhomie to make his way in the world. Wilson's stage directions describe him as a man who "fancies himself a musician [but] is more caught up in the rituals and 'idea' of being a musician than in the actual practice of the music." While this may be true, Lyons expresses sentiments about his music that recall Ma Rainey's comments about the blues:

> LYONS: I need something that gonna help me get out of the bed in the morning. Make me feel like I belong in the world. I don't bother nobody. I just stay with my music cause that's the only way I can find to live in the world. Otherwise there ain't no telling what I might do. (18)

Behind his nonchalant, cheery mask, Lyons is just another confused black man dealing with a difficult world as best he knows how. His indolence is more the symptom than the disease. He did not have a Troy Maxson to push and prod him, to discipline him, to lecture him, to somehow beat a work ethic into him. Cory had that and, although he strained at the leash, absorbed enough of his father's strength of purpose and discipline to be a success in the marines. Lyons, raised in poverty by his mother and lacking the fortitude to make the up-hill climb, takes the easy way out. Such a lifestyle carries a high social price, and Lyons finally pays it—three years in the workhouse. Only then, in prison, does he decide to turn his life around. Thus, Troy's sons find their identities in different ways. Cory transcends his anger and frustration to master the system; Lyons slips between the cracks of the system and then shows signs of wanting to pick himself up and start again, just as his father did. From his father he learned to "take the crookeds with the straights" and use them to create his own survival kit. An important part of that kit is the music that will sustain him in the years ahead. The blues will help him find his true self. It will help him survive. And he will survive—he is, after all, his father's son.

Of all the characters in this play, Bono seems the most well adjusted. His character is the foil against which Troy's philosophy of life, his lifestyle itself, and his personality are reflected. He met Troy in prison, and they settled into a long friendship. We get the impression that the two important things that happened to Troy in prison were his association with Bono and his discovery of baseball. These two events certainly have exerted a strong influence on his life. Troy spends more time with Bono than he does with anyone else. They work together, engage in weekly rituals of drinking, chatting, and domino-playing; and their families are close friends. While Troy finds it hard to display any feelings of affection for his family, he easily tells Bono that he loves him. They have a special relationship, having been with each other through the good times and the bad. Bono knows Troy almost as well as Rose does. At the beginning of the play he is wary of his friend's growing relationship with Alberta, almost before Troy is aware that he is being drawn into something that will get out of control. Bono even knows Rose well. When Troy and Cory complain about her desire for a fence, it is Bono who understands her motives.

We never see Bono's wife, Lucille, but the two of them obviously have a strong relationship. They have weathered the hard times and built a comfortable nook in which to grow old together. The hallmarks of Bono's character are comfort and contentment. He asks little from life except a steady job and the warmth of his relationships with his wife and friends. His contentment provides a marked contrast to Troy's edginess. By the same token, he lacks the ambition of his friend and has no active desire to change his lifestyle. Early in the play, Bono says that he did not want to have children because he "didn't know if [he] was gonna be in one place long enough to fix on them right as their daddy." Having had a father who was a wanderer, he is afraid to do the same to his children. It is ironic that Bono, who appears to be a settled family man, has no children, while Troy, with his roving eye and restless spirit, has three. But having children is not necessarily a social decision. In Troy's case, it is the result of an innate procreative urge—the same prerogative commanded by his mythological ancestor, the phallocentric trickster.

Bono lets Troy take the lead; he is happy to admire and follow. He also has a high regard for Rose and chides Troy for his affair with Alberta. Troy's relationship with Rose is important to Bono, for he sees his own life and marriage as a reflection of his friend's. But two things happen almost simultaneously to drive a wedge between them. First, Troy's affair with Alberta grows stronger, and he spends more time away from his family and friend. Second, Troy gets his promotion, is assigned to hauling white folks' garbage, and no longer works with Bono. In yet another example of separation as a prerequisite for the establishment of one's freedom, Troy's promotion lead to a further separation from his friend. Bono complains that, in his new position, Troy "ain't got to do nothing but sit up there and read the paper like them white fellows." And later, as he talks about his new life, there is a wistful note in Troy's voice: "It ain't the same, Bono. It ain't like working the back of the truck. Ain't got nobody to talk to. . . . feel like you working by yourself" (83). For this black man in a white man's job, life is lonely. The closer he gets to white society the more he is isolated from his people.

For a major portion of the play, Troy is engaged in building a fence round his yard. Bono suggests that Rose wants him to build it so she can keep her family safe from the forces that threaten the stability she has worked so hard to maintain. When she met Troy, Rose was like Dussie Mae in *Ma Rainey*—in search of security in a relationship. Unlike Dussie Mae, however, she refused to settle for anything less than permanent. The product of a broken home, she was not looking for a sexual partner but a husband and a family. Once she got her family she focused all her energies on keeping it together. She is a wife and mother, cooking and keeping house for them; she is the buffer between Cory and Troy, striving to turn their anger into understanding and love. She assuages Troy's guilt over Gabe, keeps his bed warm, and his libido satisfied. She even cares for his illegitimate daughter. She does all this because her family means everything to her. It defines her very existence, and without it she would be lost.

Rose knows she is married to a restless man and must find ways to keep him near her. Bono is right about the symbolism of the fence—she wants to keep her family in and the world out. Her constant prayer is for security. But Troy delays building the fence, as though fearful of the restrictions it will place on him. Something within him rebels against the idea of being cut off from the world, of having no escape from the pressures of family life. Although he loves Rose, the daily grind of providing for his family for eighteen years has left little room for joy, and he seeks relief in the arms of a mistress. Perhaps, subconsciously, Troy feels that the fence, while keeping his family within, might also keep him away from Alberta. With her, he can look beyond his social role as a breadwinner and revel in the phallocentric realm of his mythic ancestors, celebrating the freedom of his emotions and satisfying his need for laughter and sexual release. But self-empowerment, even in the mythic sense, comes at an enormous social price: it costs him his relationship with his wife.

When questioned about his affair with Alberta, Troy refers to it metaphorically as his attempt to steal second base after staying on first all his life. For one brief moment, he feels he can make it, but after a perilous sprint, he is thrown out by Death. Suddenly, he finds himself stranded between bases—with a dead mistress at one end, a wronged wife at the other, and himself in the middle—literally holding the baby. Faced with the specter of a final separation from Rose and his family, Troy decides to finish the fence. With Alberta gone, he desperately tries to huddle closer to whatever is left of his family.

But almost as soon as Troy finishes the fence that will keep his family safe, he has a fight with Cory, who then threatens to leave. As his son walks away, Troy tells him he will find his things "on the other side of that fence." The fence thus becomes a symbol of separation in this play and underscores the complex role this theme plays in Troy's life. At the beginning, it took him away from the slavery of the farm toward a new role as a free man; at the end, it cuts him off from his family and friends. Ironically, the more freedom he achieves, the lonelier he becomes. For the trickster in search of self-authentication, the exercise of individual will leads him down a lonely path.

When Troy confesses his affair, Rose's whole world begins to crumble. Suddenly, everything she has worked for is in danger of collapsing. For years, she submerged her personality to stand by her husband and build a home, putting her personal dreams on hold to let her husband and children grow. But now she realizes her mistake in not asserting herself more. Her self-effacement allowed Troy to take her for granted; by giving him her strength, she weakened herself. Years later, at Troy's funeral, she reveals this to Cory:

> I married your daddy and settled down to cooking his supper and keeping clean sheets on the bed. When your daddy walked through the house he was so big he filled it up. That was my first mistake. Not to make him leave some room for me. For my part in the matter. I didn't know that to keep up his strength I had to give up little pieces of mine. I did that. I took on his life as mine and mixed up the pieces so that you couldn't hardly tell which was which anymore. (98)

By investing her dreams, her hopes, and her personality in her husband, she neglected an essential part of herself. Now she has very little left to call her own.

Troy's betrayal launches Rose on a search for her own self-affirmation. Once again, separation from a dear one sets the stage for this journey as she elbows him aside to make room for herself. She does not give up her marriage immediately. For six months she maintains an emotional distance from Troy, awaiting his next move. She also uses this time to bathe her wounds and renew her strength. Once she sees that Troy will not give up Alberta, she confronts him with an ultimatum. However much she may need this marriage or her family, Rose is too honest and forthright to live a lie. At this moment, fate intervenes—Alberta dies in childbirth—saving Rose from the disastrous decision of rejecting the family that has defined her. Levee and Troy both have rejected the things that defined them and are left spiritually stranded.[8] Rose stands in the same danger, but fate rescues her. It also brings her husband back to her.

With the psychological rift between them too deep to be bridged completely, Troy cannot ever regain the full relationship he once had with his wife, for now Rose knows that Troy Maxson is not her only way to self-fulfillment; she can achieve the full stature of her true identity without sacrificing her womanhood to him. Fate, or chance, which worked so often against her, presents her with a solution to her dilemma. It gives her new life in the form of a baby.

By taking in Troy's baby daughter, Rose becomes a mother once more. Years later, she will say to Cory that she married only to fill some of the empty spaces in her life, and "one of them empty spaces was being somebody's mother." Betrayed as a wife, she puts that role aside and embraces motherhood again. This decision also gives her the freedom to find new channels for her energies, and she involves herself in activities at her church. She does not leave Troy but continues to be the woman of the house, though that is more an extension of her role as a mother than as a wife. As she says to Cory later, "By the time Raynell came into the house, me and your daddy had lost touch with one another. I didn't want to make my blessing off of nobody's misfortune . . . but I took on to Raynell like she was all them babies I had wanted and never had. Like I'd been blessed to relive a part of my life. And if the lord see fit to keep up my strength . . . I'm gonna do her just like your daddy did you. . . . I'm gonna give her the best of what's in me" (98).

It would never have occurred to Rose to do other than what she did. During slavery, the destruction of families and forced separations engendered among black people a sense of community that extended its sheltering embrace to every destitute person of the community. Whoever needed a home received it as a matter of course. No one was without a family; everyone belonged to the community. In this case, the child needed a mother and found one.

In this play, the search for identity by blacks is an exploration of their individual characteristics, their mythic signification, and their struggle to integrate with society. But, as society is made up of various institutions, this quest for their freedom may be a process of institutionalization, which is itself a kind of separation. At the end of *Fences,* all the characters are in some kind of institution. Cory has joined the marines and is about to get married; Lyons is nearing the end of his term at the workhouse; Rose is heavily involved with her church; Gabriel is in the hospital; Bono remains married to Lucille; and Raynell now has a family. Troy is uncontainable, except by death. While institutions tend to curb the individual's freedom, they also have the potential to be a source of strength. Lyons turns his life around and faces the future with optimism. Gabriel is being cared for and finally gets his big moment when he sees the gates of heaven open for Troy, for himself, and for whoever wants to follow.

Fences is therefore an odyssey of survival. Troy Maxson finds himself on the brink of a new society, and his past experiences force him to distrust the promise of change and to pursue, instead, his own idea of freedom. Although some of his actions appear to be sanctioned within the realm of his mythological forebears, his quest for personal authentication and his struggle to protect his family compel him to negotiate the realities of a society essentially at odds with his cultural past. Against these turbulent crosscurrents, Troy discovers that individual freedom inevitably involves separation, and he often finds himself cut off from the family he is trying to safeguard—from Lyons because he was in prison during the boy's youth; from Rose because of his affair with Alberta; and from Cory for refusing him permission to accept a football scholarship. But this initial alienation ultimately leads each to individual empowerment because, first, Troy's actions propel them toward their own destinies in the new emerging society and, second, they learn to accept his actions as a consequence of his struggle to save himself and them from destruction.

The end of the play is set in 1965. The 1964 Civil Rights Act was the most promising of all the civil rights legislation to date; it included the establishment of the Equal Employment Opportunity Commission, the first real glimmer of hope in almost a century of freedom. Reflecting this optimism is Troy Maxson's legacy to his family: each of them has been endowed with his strength of purpose. Despite his flaws, or, perhaps, because of them, he taught his family how to "take the straights with the crookeds"; to recognize and play to their strengths; "not to make the same mistakes . . . to take life as it comes along and keep putting one foot in front of the other." As all of them move toward their individual and collective destinies, they have a surer sense of who they are and a greater instinct for survival because of Troy Maxson.

3

JOE TURNER'S COME AND GONE

SEEK AND YOU SHALL FIND

Once the Reconstruction era ended in 1877 and the South was "redeemed" by its white majority, it became clear that the new society would do its best to regain what it had lost with the war and the Emancipation Proclamation. This new phase began with the "withdrawal of federal troops from the South, the abandonment of the Negro as a ward of the nation, the giving up of the attempt to guarantee the freedman his civil and political equality, and the acquiescence of the rest of the country in the South's demand that the whole problem be left to the disposition of the dominant Southern white people" (Woodward 6). Thus, long before the turn of the century when segregation became a legal fact, the social and economic restructuring of the South precluded any progress toward full citizenship for black people and paved the way for the Jim Crow laws of the early twentieth century.

In shocked reaction to the realization that the prize they had sought for so long was now being snatched away just as it was within reach, some blacks struck out for the North. One of the first states to attract them was Kansas, but as northern employers began removing the color bar restricting jobs to whites, the exodus to Kansas soon spread to other industrial cities. This northern migration was a slow process, for blacks were still reluctant to place themselves in the hands of people who had left them at the mercy of their former owners. In 1830, 92.8 percent of the total black population of America lived in the South; by 1910, that number had decreased to just 89 percent (Grant 13)—not much of difference. It was not until the Jim Crow laws went into effect that blacks really began their great migration. During the next two decades—from 1910 to 1930—the black population doubled and trebled in Philadelphia, Pittsburgh, Chicago, and New York (Grant 28).

In *Fences*, August Wilson portrays the effects of this migration forty years later, that is, the continuing struggle to find jobs and hold together disintegrating families and homes. In *Joe Turner's Come and Gone*, Wilson returns to the beginning of the southern exodus and explores the genesis of what was really a journey toward self-affirmation. He depicts the influence of the migration on the identity of each character: how their quests for lost loves and new loves reflect a deeper search for themselves. He then raises fundamental questions about the nature of the black experience in America, probing the fascinating blend of two cultures that have informed the sensibilities of black Americans—their African heritage and the Christian tradition into which they were thrust. Wilson investigates their poignant yearnings for meaningful relationships and their struggle to sing the song of their true identity. While in *Fences* Wilson focuses on the continuing effects of separation and migration in the lives of black people during the 1950s, in *Joe Turner* he deals with the ways in which separation and migration launched the twentieth-century destinies of blacks in urban America. In both plays, the path to self-discovery lies in a reunion with the past, a solution he continues to explore and advocate in his next play, *The Piano Lesson*.

Although the story line of *Joe Turner* follows Herald Loomis's search for his lost wife, its underlying action is his odyssey toward self-empowerment. Set in a boardinghouse in Pittsburgh—run by Seth and Bertha Holly—the play begins in 1911, at the start of the decade in which began the massive influx of southern blacks into northern cities.[1] Significantly, 1911 was the year in which the National League on Urban Conditions among Negroes[2] (later called the National Urban League) was founded, for the play focuses on the first tentative efforts of blacks to adapt to urban life.

Seth Holly is in an unusual position for an urban black. He owns a boardinghouse, was "born of Northern free parents, is a skilled craftsman . . . and has a stability that none of the other characters [has]." This stability becomes more apparent when reflected against the disjointed lifestyles of those around him. His marriage of over twenty-five years is surrounded by broken relationships, and his trade as a tinsmith gives him a solidity that contrasts sharply with the confused meanderings of the others. Indeed, Seth is one of the most socially stable of all Wilson's characters. Even Ma Rainey lived an itinerant life, taking her act from town to town, aware that her power derived only from her continued popularity with her audience. Seth, on the other hand, has put down roots in Pittsburgh and has three sources of income—his job with Mr. Olowski, his business with Rutherford Selig, and the boardinghouse. While he pays a stiff price for his stability—working nights for Olowski and days to keep his enterprise with Selig profitable—it has made him a little intolerant toward those of his race who are less enterprising. He drives a hard bargain with prospective boarders, demands payment in advance, and is impatient with any behavior alien to his work ethic. Bynum's rituals are dismissed as "old mumbo jumbo nonsense" and "that heebie-jeebie stuff," and Jeremy's brushes with the law draw from Seth a scathing denouncement of blacks who have migrated from the South. His disdain springs from the fact that, as a child of free northern parents, he has no firsthand knowledge of life on the plantation and cannot sympathize with the special need to get away from the roots and locale of slavery.

Seth's anger is directed against what he perceives to be the naïveté of migrating blacks in leaving the safety of their southern farms to journey north without any knowledge of the hostile social climate they will encounter. Southern blacks were rural folk, at home on the farm. The cities of the North thrust them out of their element, forcing them to compete for jobs with whites from all over the world, immigrants from other lands seeking a similar freedom. These pre–World War I years were witness to another great migration—from Europe to the new world of the Americas. This movement, trickling along for over a hundred years, had accelerated near the turn of the century and was gathering force until the clouds of war loomed ominously over Europe.

In *Fences,* we saw that freedom for blacks meant rootlessness, a severance from their homes and families. European immigrants were also forced to uproot themselves to achieve economic freedom and, in the case of Jews, freedom from persecution and death. As these two waves of immigrants flooded America in search of new beginnings, the racial climate favored the Caucasian.

Seth knows that in the scramble for a piece of the urban pie, blacks invariably come up short. Like Troy Maxson, he is painfully aware that blacks come to the plate with two strikes against them, and every moment thereafter is an agonizing struggle just to stay in the game, let alone win. While Seth has a firm sense of his social role as a black northern businessman, he realizes this security is tenuous: it has to be reaffirmed every day. Working almost twenty-four hours is not enough: "I can't get nowhere working for Mr. Olowski and selling Selig five or six pots on the side." All his attempts at borrowing money to launch his own business fail because his would-be creditors demand his house as collateral. These are unacceptable terms for, at a time when most urban blacks live in shanties and slums, this house is a unique symbol of his stability. It is his home and his business asset. It belonged to his father and stands as an emblem of the success and security of his position as a family man and entrepreneur.

If life is so difficult for a black man born and raised in the city, it is virtually devastating for credulous black migrants without the street wisdom to survive in an urban jungle. Jeremy Furlough is one such yokel who falls easy prey to city predators like the police, who have their own methods of reducing the overpopulated streets—rounding up black men like cattle, arresting them, and herding them off the streets. When Jeremy is fired from his job because he will not yield to a white man's efforts to extort part of his salary, Molly tells him it will be easy to get his job back. He has only to return the next day and sign up again, for no one will recognize him as the man who was fired the day before—to urban whites blacks are just an anonymous horde of nameless, faceless people without any social identity or individuality, as indistinguishable from one another as animals in a field.

Rutherford Selig is another white man who exploits the desperate circumstances of migrant blacks. Known as the People Finder, he keeps a list of his customers as they move about. Though he appears to be working in the service of the myriad groups of blacks searching for family and friends, his exorbitant fee of one dollar[3] belies any altruistic motives. Bertha claims he is a fraud who never really finds someone he did not take away in the first place. It is true that Selig finds Martha Pentecost, but the fact that she used to stay at the boardinghouse suggests she probably left with him and that Bertha is right about his methods. Selig is the last in a long line of white pursuers, making a profit of finding black people:

> we been finders in my family for a long time. Bringers and finders. My great-grandaddy used to bring Nigras across the ocean on ships. . . . Me and my daddy have found plenty of Nigras. My daddy, rest his soul, used to find runaway slaves for the plantation bosses. . . . After Abraham Lincoln give you all Nigras your freedom papers and with you all looking all over for each other . . . we started finding Nigras for Nigras. Of course, it don't pay as much. But the People Finding business ain't so bad. (41)

The disruption of black communities that began with forced migrations from Africa and the selling of slaves piecemeal from plantation to plantation thus continues in a new cycle as sharecropping drives them from their homes in search of a better environment. This, ironically, maintains the profitability of trading in blacks, and Rutherford Selig has found an innovative way to continue the family tradition by finding black people separated as a consequence of slavery and sharecropping.

The rhythms of slavery are thus kept alive in various ways: Joe Turner, the brother of the governor of Tennessee, blithely ignores the law and enslaves blacks on his farm; every seven years his men scour the countryside to capture blacks for his chain gang. Mr. Piney and his policemen use the law to imprison innocent blacks and extort money from them. And Rutherford Selig, in the guise of a benefactor, keeps alive a three-hundred-year-old business of black trading by profiteering from the circumstances that forced them into separation and migration.

Wilson sets this play in a boardinghouse, a temporary shelter for people on their way to something else, and all the characters who come by are searching for something or someone. Most of them have been separated from a loved one and have traveled long journeys to fill their emptiness. Loomis is looking for his wife, Martha, after spending seven years of enforced labor on a chain gang in Tennessee. With his daughter, he has "been out there walking up and down [the] roads," not sure where he will meet up with Martha, but determined to find her, however long it takes. Mattie needs Bynum to help her find her man, Jack Carper. And Bynum is searching for the shiny man he once met in an apocalyptic experience. Even the children learn early that separation and migration are a way of life. When Zonia tells Reuben that they have to leave, his dissatisfaction is pointed: "Dag! You just only been here for a little while. Don't seem like nothing ever stay the same." He senses that he belongs to a dislocated people. "You mine. . . . when I get grown, I come looking for you," he tells Zonia. Thus, a new generation of black people will continue the tradition of looking for loved ones. Searching is second nature to Zonia, for she has known virtually no other life. When Loomis gives her to Martha she clings to him pathetically, crying for the loss of quests without end: "I won't get no bigger! My bones won't get no bigger! They won't! I promise! Take me with you till we keep searching and never finding" (91).

Throughout the play, there is much mention of roads and traveling. Jeremy works on a road gang and we are told about the numerous roads being built all over the country. As long as there are roads, blacks will travel:

> SETH: . . . these niggers keep on coming. Walking . . . riding . . . carrying their Bibles. That boy done carried a guitar all the way from North Carolina. What he gonna find out? What he gonna do with that guitar? This is the city. Niggers come up here from the backwoods . . . coming up here from the country carrying Bibles and guitars looking for freedom. (6)

With a Bible and a guitar they have religion and the blues, their most potent symbols of hope. By 1911, the blues was just starting to become popular as a musical form. In its rhythms blacks recognized not only the echoes of slave worksongs but also the hopes and fears of three hundred years of slavery, reaching back all the way to the music of Africa. In their darkest moments they found comfort in the blues, the one steadfast thing in this restless world of flux and uncertainty. It was always there whenever they needed it. "Music don't know no certain night," says Bynum, referring to Seefus's bar where black folk congregate to make the music that unites them with a common bond and keeps them in touch with their deepest roots. It permitted spiritual and emotional release by codifying their experiences and was a testament to the fact that they were not a disparate bunch of wandering souls but descendants from and inheritors of a rich and fascinating tradition. The blues set them apart, for it was alien to the sensibilities of white people, as illustrated by Jeremy's story about a white man's inability to tell the difference between two blues musicians. Ma Rainey expressed similar sentiments: "White folks don't understand about the blues. They hear it come out, but they don't know how it got there. They don't understand that's life's way of talking" (*Ma Rainey* 82). The music filled the lives of blacks with purpose, and for that they would risk anything. "Some things is worth taking the chance going to jail about."

This period of their history, with its ceaseless quests, finds special meaning in lyrics that tell of loneliness and the search for companionship. In a haunting blues poem, "Bound No'th Blues," Langston Hughes captures this emotion with great poignancy:

> Road's in front o' me,
> Nothin' to do but walk.
> Road's in front o' me,
> Walk . . . and walk . . . and walk.
> I'd like to meet a good friend
> To come along an' talk. (quoted in Grant 48–49)

As long as he has the blues, Jeremy can set off down the road and go where it takes him. "I can get my guitar and always find me a place to stay." Migration and the motives that prompted it are typified in the peripatetic lifestyle of blues singers. Robert Palmer underscores this in an episode about two famous bluesmen, Robert Johnson and Johnny Shines:

> [They] began traveling together, hitching rides, hopping freight trains, perpetually on the move from somewhere to somewhere else. "Robert was a guy, you could wake him up any time and he was ready to *go*," Shines says. "Say, for instance, you had come from Memphis to Helena, and we'd play there all night probably and lay down to sleep the next morning and hear a train. You say, 'Robert, I hear a train. Let's catch it.' He wouldn't exchange no words with you. He's just ready to go. We'd go right back to Memphis if that's where the train's going. It didn't make him no difference. Just so he was going." (118)

Having been tied down for so long by slavery and sharecropping, blacks were anxious to be on the move, unable to put down roots just yet, desperate to fill a spiritual void created by three hundred years of captivity. Blues lyrics spoke of this desire to get away and reflected the separation behind the migration: men and women looking for each other or leaving their homes and their loved ones. There was also a fascination with travel for its own sake that was rooted in the years of black captivity (Palmer 20). For decades, the urge to escape or even to travel had been curbed, but now that free movement was comparatively easy, many blacks saw migration as the only way to maintain their sanity. The transition from their old social identities as slaves to their new identities as free people lay in the very act of wandering, which in itself was a step toward self-empowerment, a reaffirmation of their freedom to go where they pleased without permits or permission. Ironically, as illustrated in *Fences,* freedom meant rootlessness, even being cut off from their new roots in the South.[4]

In this play, the apparent endlessness of each quest appears to be connected to the nature of the separation that launched the search. In every case, it occurred under circumstances over which the searchers had no control, so now they do not know where the person they are searching for might possibly be. Loomis was snatched by Joe

Turner's men while in the middle of a roadside sermon; Mattie's husband blamed her for the loss of their two babies and walked away; Jeremy's girl left without a word: "Woke up one morning and she was gone. Just took off to parts unknown." Because the estrangements occurred without any presage, the very suddenness of the acts has left their egos shattered, not in the superficial sense of their pride being hurt, but in the more profound sense of a spiritual dislocation. An essential part of themselves is lost, and they will never be whole again until it is replaced.

Each quest, therefore, seems like a crusade in search of something more intangible and mystical than just another person, a journey that is as much inward as outward—a spiritual exploration of the psyche that finds expression in a physical exploration of the country. They are all, in one way or another, looking for themselves. The innumerable references to roads, traveling, feet, and shoes—as well as the constant coming and going of characters in and out of this temporary shelter—create the effect of a restless world beyond the boardinghouse, a world of other people on the move as well. Against this backdrop, these characters appear as archetypes reflecting countless blacks in similar circumstances—a whole race of people somewhere out there on a pilgrimage toward self-fulfillment.

Bynum calls this quest the search for one's song: "See, Mr. Loomis, when a man forgets his song he goes off in search of it . . . till he find out he's got it with him all the time." Without this song people are doomed to wander through life aimlessly, unaware of who they are or what their purpose may be. This song is the music of each person's essential nature, his or her true identity. And that identity, with its special rhythms, dictates the course of each one's destiny. Each song is unique, with its unique power that derives from the unique mix of each person's characteristics. Bynum has the Binding Song, his father had the Healing Song. Both were healers, however—the father made individuals whole, the son does the same for relationships. But for a man to touch the lives of other men, he must first be in tune with his own song.

Bynum was shown the way to his song by the shiny man and the spirit of his father. Wilson describes him as giving "the impression of always being in control of everything. Nothing ever bothers him. He seems to be lost in a world of his own making and to swallow any adversity or interference with his grand design." Having found his song, his life's work now is to help others find their songs. He chose the Binding Song "because that's what [he saw] most when [he] was traveling . . . people walking away and leaving one another." He looked around at a fractured race of wandering people and knew he had to spend his life healing the wounds caused by shattered relationships, bringing together these people dispersed by chance and circumstance. His search for the shiny man is different from the other quests. Having found his mission, his energies are spent in its service. All he needs now is another shiny man to place the seal of approval on his work, to corroborate his belief that his true identity is indeed that of a mender of broken relationships. But even he has had his share of wandering: "I wore many a pair of shoes out walking around that way. You'd have thought I was a missionary spreading the gospel the way I wandered all around them parts" (42).

Bynum is a rootworker, a conjurer with a special connection to nature. His strength derives from a tradition that stretches directly back through slavery to his African roots. He is a highly evolved descendant of the medicine man of African tribes and the conjurer of slave plantations.[5] Many of his predecessors sought power by instilling fear in their charges, but Bynum's demeanor is one of compassion, love, and sensitivity. In *Roll, Jordan, Roll,* Eugene D. Genovese describes this evolution of conjurers from an instrument of evil to an instrument of good:

Conjurers might be evildoers; they might be people who, like the witches of the European persecutions, had been wronged themselves and sought revenge on mankind. In either case, fear had to be their weapon, for even a good deed for one person normally had to come at the expense of someone else. Down to our own time, hoodoo doctors, not being fools, have studied their people and learned how to provide them with advice designed to produce results an expensive psychoanalyst might envy. They have put this talent to particular use in their work as "root doctors" and have thereby performed the closest thing to an unambiguously positive service. (223–24)

Bynum owes his mythological ancestry to the Ifa tradition—whose presiding deity is Orunmila—in Yoruban cosmology. His sharply tuned intuition appears to endow him with the gift of divination, particularly when it comes to sensing which relationships need consolidation. His is the oracular voice from which the other characters seek affirmation and solutions, the steadying influence in this world of upheaval. Clara Odugbesan describes Ifa "not as a deity to be worshipped, but as an oracle from which people try to obtain certainty from uncertainty in any human problem ranging from the choice of a chief or a king from among prospective candidates, to the choice of a husband or a site for a building, or the request for the gift of a child" (202). There is a significant difference between Eshu and Ifa, as Odugbesan points out:

> The roles of Eshu and Ifa within the cosmological system of ideas are diametrically opposed to one another. Ifa is a system whose function is to promote orderliness in the world, one that corrects all wrongs by mediating between men and gods for good, and produces certainty where there is uncertainty. Eshu, on the other hand, is associated with disorderliness and confusion. . . . Both Eshu and Ifa mediate between men and their gods; but while one (Eshu) disrupts relationship between them, the other consolidates it. (201)

These two traditions that operate simultaneously within the African cosmology are to be found at the heart of many cultures—Apollo and Dionysius in ancient Greece, Vishnu and Siva in Hindu mythology,[6] Yin and Yang in Chinese philosophy. Each of them alone would present a one-dimensional world of either order or chaos. Together they furnish the complexities of life and living that derive from daily renegotiations of the very oppositions represented by them. In fact, the term opposition is almost a misnomer; rather, they appear to be complementary entities in a complex cultural system. Odugbesan clarifies:

> Yoruba legends depict great rivalry between Eshu and Orunmila, Eshu claiming the right to hide people in misfortune, while Orunmila offers them certainty through divination and sacrifice. What appears a more logical conclusion is that the world comprehended and revealed by Orunmila has uncertainties ascribed to inter-

vention by Eshu, who has to be reckoned with. Hence Ifa, the cult of Orunmila, is operated hand in hand with ritual observances for Eshu. (201)

Loomis, as we will later see, is a mythological descendant of Eshu, the same tradition that spurred Levee and Troy. It is natural that he and Bynum finally achieve individual authentication only by working together. August Wilson's world, therefore, is peopled with manifestations of both systems—Eshu and Ifa—each bringing its own special character to the negotiation table as they reach for individual affirmation and collective rapprochement. The Levees and Troy Maxsons are as important and necessary as the Bynums, for in their interaction they validate not only themselves but each other.

Bynum brings an intense commitment to his work, taking time and effort to study the particulars of each case. In the best tradition of a true missionary, he becomes deeply involved with the person he is trying to help: "Oh, I don't do it lightly. It cost me a piece of myself every time I do. I'm a Binder of What Clings. You got to find out if they cling first. You can't bind what don't cling" (10). He does not see himself as a creator of relationships but as a catalyst helping to join only those people who were meant to be together. He is thus an agent of fate in the service of the cosmic forces that bind and loose people. He tells Mattie Campbell that he can put a spell on Jack Carper to return, but he warns against bringing back a person who "ain't supposed to come back. . . . And if he ain't supposed to come back . . . then he'll be in your bed one morning and it'll come up on him that he's in the wrong place. That he's lost outside of time from his place that he's supposed to be in. Then both of you be lost and trapped outside of life and ain't no way for you to get back into it" (22).

In this dismembered world of ex-slaves only the healthy relationships are worth preserving. The search for one's song is a quest for spiritual transcendence, a sensitive journey into the innermost depths of one's being in pursuit of self-affirmation. Such a voyage can be undertaken only by people truly committed to each other, companions compatible enough to foster, not inhibit, the surge toward fulfillment. The bad blood between Mattie and Jack over the loss of their babies has severed forever his destiny from hers, and his path now leads him to someone else.

Like Rose in *Fences,* Mattie is completely obsessed with her man. Her description of Jack and their relationship ("Seem like he's the strongest man in the world the way he hold me") echoes Rose's description of Troy at the end of *Fences* ("here is a man that you can open yourself up to and be filled to bursting"). Mattie's vulnerability is enhanced by her guilt over the loss of the infants because Jack told her that someone had placed a curse on her. In an effort to erase that terrible memory she could easily become a slave to her husband. Like Rose, Mattie would then find no room for her own individuality and identity. She is a desperate woman, and desperate women either get swallowed up by the relationship, as Rose did, or, as Jeremy declares, they inadvertently push their men away.

Bynum intuitively knows that Mattie's relationship with Jack is potentially destructive and that her only hope is to break free. As in *Fences,* here too separation is the first step toward self-fulfillment. Just as Rose was forced to do, Mattie must make room in her life for herself. Rose could do so and remain in the same house with Troy because in their case a newborn child was there and they needed to provide for it together. In Mattie's case, her two children are dead and there is nothing to bind her to Jack. Somehow she needs to separate herself from him just as he has separated himself from her. Bynum offers her the following advice: "Ain't no need you fretting over Jack Carper. Right now he's a strong thought in your mind. But every time you catch yourself fretting over Jack Carper you push that thought away. You push it out your mind and that thought will get weaker and weaker till you wake up one morning and you won't even be able to call him up on your mind" (24). He knows this is difficult for Mattie to accomplish on her own. Autosuggestion and other psychoanalytic methods work well enough, but Bynum, reaching deep into Mattie's African roots for more tangible succor for the anxiety ahead, gives her a charm to help push Jack Carper from her mind. Before offering the solution or the talisman, he hints that she may soon find a replacement for her lost husband: "Jack Carper gone off to where he belong. There's somebody searching for your doorstep right now."

It seems almost inevitable that Jeremy would step in to woo Mattie. Since his girl left him, he has been in search of love and companionship from town to town, aware that in this uncertain world very little is guaranteed or permanent. With not much more than his guitar, he feels the need to keep on the move, going where the road leads him. But Mattie is weary of being on the go for so long. Like other women in Wilson's plays—especially Dussie Mae and Rose—she wants to settle down, to link her fate with one man in a lasting relationship. Though the setbacks in her search for companionship have dimmed her optimism, they have not shaken her faith in the possibility of love. With Bynum's advice in her ears and his charm in her pocket, she is willing to take yet another chance on love, even though Jeremy is not exactly her kindred spirit. Her interest peaks when she learns that he is a guitar player—the blues may be just what her bruised spirits need, and if this man can bring the blues to her she will put out the welcome mat once more.

If Mattie is a forerunner of those Wilson women in search of a permanent relationship, Jeremy is the youthful personification of the men they seem fated to meet—men like Levee and Troy—descendants of the procreative trickster—who seek sexual gratification as their prerogative. As soon as Mattie agrees to see Jeremy, he makes his real intentions known in metaphors reminiscent of Levee's sexual boasts: "I plays [the guitar], sugar, and that ain't all I do. I got a ten-pound hammer and I knows how to drive it down. Good god . . . you ought to hear my hammer ring!" (26). Bynum tries to explain to Jeremy that a woman is not a sex object ("You just can't look at a woman to jump off into bed with her") but a true companion made in the image of his mother. He says that a woman is like land to a man stranded on the great waterways of life: she can be all he will ever need if he learns to set his rhythms in harmony with hers. Bynum seems to be suggesting that men will never find their true identity, their song, unless they can make room in their world for women to find theirs, for the destinies of men and women are inextricably linked, as surely as sons are shaped and influenced by their mothers.

But Jeremy and Mattie are not traveling in the same spiritual direction. They are essentially different, with different sensibilities and different goals. She wants to settle down, but he has to travel. Bynum immediately senses this incompatibility. He knows they are not meant to be together. When Jeremy announces him that Mattie is going to move in with him, Bynum's cryptic remark suggests that he thinks she could be making a mistake: "Sometimes you got to be where you supposed to be. Sometimes you can get all mixed up in life and come to the wrong place" (45).

When Molly Cunningham appears, Jeremy takes to her almost as soon as he meets her. This is the kind of woman Bynum was talking about, the land on his horizon. The antithesis of Mattie Campbell's reticence, Molly's independent spirit revolts against all the things Mattie holds dear. She too is the product of a broken relationship, but her experience has hardened her against trusting "[anybody] but the good Lord above, and [loving anybody] but mama." Having seen her mother enslaved by babies and household chores, she is determined to avoid the familial trap—marriage is potential slavery and motherhood would cramp her style.

Molly's search for self-authentication has brought her on a journey as far from her childhood roots as possible. Available for a relationship only on her terms, she tells Jeremy that she will not work, cannot be bought, and will not go south. He finds this roving spirit attractive, seeing in her self-assertiveness the promise of seasoned adventure. She is a free soul, quite able to take care of herself, certainly not one of the desperate women he sought to avoid. Maybe she can be the companion an itinerant bluesman needs. Both are looking for companionship but neither wants to be tied to one place. So they join the throngs that wander along the roads and byways from town to town, "their heart kicking in their chest with a song worth singing . . . seeking . . . a new identity as free men [and women] of definite and sincere worth" (Introduction).

If Mattie and Molly are searching for meaningful relationships, albeit along different paths, Bertha seems to have found what she wants out of life. In her comfortable marriage, she has learned to "negotiate around Seth's apparent orneriness." Her key to happiness is a trouble-free mind, and she offers this advice to Mattie when Jeremy leaves: "Don't no man want a woman with a troubled mind. You get all that trouble off your mind and just when it look like you ain't never gonna find what you want . . . you look up and it's standing right there. That's how I met my Seth. You gonna look up one day and find everything you want standing right in front of you. Been twenty-seven years now since that happened to me" (75). Bertha presides over the play like a mother figure, cooking and cleaning, advising someone here, admonishing another there, acting as a lightning rod to diffuse Seth's anger at Loomis, consoling Mattie when Jeremy leaves her, taking Zonia under her wing, directing Loomis to another boardinghouse. It is significant that most of the action takes place in her kitchen, a milieu in which she is most at home. This underscores the importance of her nurturing presence, which acts as a calming influence on the often frantic scurrying about that occurs there.

Bertha's strength derives from a blend of two religious traditions perfectly synthesized in her abundant spirit. On the same morning she can go to church like a good Christian and then return home to sprinkle salt all over the house as a protection against evil spirits[7] or line her threshold with pennies to keep witches at bay. When the aura of sadness that envelops Loomis threatens to lay a pall upon her home, she "moves about the kitchen as though blessing it . . . [with] a dance and demonstration of her own magic." Having embraced Christianity, she still remains "connected by the muscles of her heart and the blood's memory" to the music and rhythms of a "remedy that is centuries old" and a culture whose pulse continues to beat in her. It is from these ancient rhythms that she fashions an elixir for all sadness—laughter that ripples forth like a benediction from the past: "You hear me Mattie? I'm talking about laughing. The kind that comes from way deep inside. To just stand and laugh and let life flow through you. Just laugh to let yourself know you're alive" (87).

This Afro-Christianity, with its blend of ritual and prayer, has informed Bertha's deepest sensibilities and shaped her identity as an African American. Genovese discusses this blending of religious and national identities as an integral part of the evolution from slave to citizen:

The folk dynamic in the historical development of Afro-American Christianity saved the slaves from the disaster that some historians erroneously think they suffered—that of being suspended between a lost African culture and a forbidden European one. It enabled them to retain enough of Africa to help them create an appropriate form for the new content they were forging and to contribute to the mainstream of American national culture while shaping an autonomous identity. Their religion simultaneously helped build an "American" Christianity both directly and as a counterpoint and laid the foundation for a "black" Christianity of their own. That is, it made possible a universal statement because it made possible a national statement. But, for blacks, the national statement expressed a duality as something both black and American, not in the mechanical sense of being an ethnic component in a pluralistic society, but in the dialectical sense of simultaneously being itself and the other, both separately and together, and of developing as a religion within a religion in a nation within a nation. (280–81)

Joe Turner's Come and Gone is sprinkled with religious and folk images of Christianity and an African cosmology. At some points the two cultures coexist quite peacefully, as in the case of Bertha or in the image of blacks migrating from the South with their Bibles and guitars, emblems of Christianity and the African-influenced blues. On one level, Bynum, the rootworker, is an embodiment of African culture and ritual, yet his encounter with the shiny man bears potent traces of Christianity. He compares his wandering to that of a missionary spreading the gospels, and his reference to the shiny man as The One Who Goes Before and Shows the Way could also be an allusion to John the Baptist, who went before Christ and showed the way: "As it is written in the prophets, Behold, I send my messenger before thy face, which shall prepare thy way before thee" (Mark 1:2). Bynum even calls his shiny man John, "'cause it was up around Johnstown where I seen him," and the cleansing ritual conducted by the shiny man is a baptism of blood: "We get near this bend in the road and he told me to hold out my hands. Then he rubbed them together with his and I looked down and see they got blood on them.

Told me to take and rub it all over me. . . . say that was a way of cleaning myself" (9). Although John used water and promised his converts that Christ would baptize them "with the Holy Ghost and with fire" (Matt. 3:11), the true baptism that cleansed the sin of Adam and opened the gates of heaven was the baptism of the blood of Christ the Lamb.[8] "And I said unto him, Sir, thou knowest. And he said to me, These are they which came out of great tribulation, and have washed their robes, and made them white in the blood of the Lamb" (Rev. 7:14).

A more subtle Christian allusion buried in this moment refers to St. Paul's conversion (Acts 9:10–19), which, like Bynum's revelation, opened his eyes to the "Secret of Life." Both took place on a road, both were accompanied by a shining light (which blinded Paul and could have blinded Bynum), and both resulted in lifetime missions of healing. Significantly, Christ gave Peter, and, through him, all his disciples—including Paul—the Binding Power: "And I will give unto thee the keys of the kingdom of heaven; and whatsoever thou shalt bind on earth shall be bound in heaven: and whatsoever thou shalt loose on earth shall be loosed in heaven" (Matt. 16:19).

But the two cultures—African and Christian—are not always in harmony. Loomis's arrival introduces an element of tension that later deepens into physical and spiritual conflicts. In the mantle of his rebellious cultural ancestor Eshu, he lopes along the highways in a restless quest for self-validation. The stage description accompanying his entry bears an ominous note: "He is at times possessed. A man driven not by the hellhounds that seemingly bay at his heels, but by his search for a world that speaks to something about himself. He is unable to harmonize the forces that swirl around him and seeks to recreate the world into one that contains his image" (13–14). It is inevitable that such a powerful agent of change would fall foul of Seth Holly, who sees in Loomis a threat to his ordered world. Although Seth's irascible nature makes him testy with everyone, for the most part it is mere irritation, as when he gets upset with Bynum's "heebie-jeebie stuff." With Herald Loomis, it is a different matter. Having returned from the depths of hell, alienated from himself and humanity, his agonized spirit raw as a gaping wound, Loomis has an elemental aura that sets him apart, a deep sorrow that clings to him like his great coat, casting its gloom over the inn, which soon begins to quiver under his tormented gaze. A former deacon, he knows that the wife he seeks is to be found in a church, so that is where he goes. But he cannot bring himself to enter it. When Seth hears that Loomis has been seen standing outside the church, he assumes that he means to rob it.

But Loomis does not want to rob the church. If anything, the church has robbed him, for he was on church business when Joe Turner snatched him into slavery, forcing him to leave behind a wife who then "married" the Holy Ghost and changed her name to Martha Pentecost. Faint remembrances from his cultural heritage have seeped through his racial consciousness into his soul, to be confronted there with the residues of his Christian beliefs. The result is spiritual disharmony. He prowls round the church because his spirit is set to do battle with it. When the juba dance, with its African rhythms and ring shouts, builds into a frenzy and the performers yell out the name of the Holy Ghost, Loomis flies into a rage, spewing a diatribe against the Holy Ghost. The battle with Christianity has begun.

After he was snatched into slavery, Loomis began to experience the suffering of his forefathers who were stolen from their tribes. But while their captivity gave them a new religion in Christianity, his incarceration slowly stripped him of the vestiges of his adopted faith. Forced by his ordeal to confront a part of his African self, he discovers that self-empowerment can occur only with the full realization of his African identity. Standing in his way is the subverting power of his Christian self symbolized in the Holy Ghost, all the more anathematic to him because his wife has left him for the Evangelist church. The battle for his soul accelerates in the mystical climate created by the juba, and his spirit explodes at the mention of the Holy Ghost. He is hurled one way, then the other, as the subliminal struggle toward his new identity surfaces and climaxes in a pentecostal trance. As the Holy Ghost seizes hold of him, forcing him to talk in tongues, it is dispelled by a more powerful, apocalyptic experience that emerges from the depths of his subconscious past—the vision of the bones. They rise from their watery graves, march on the ocean's surface, sink down again, and, when they are finally washed ashore, Loomis sees that they are covered with flesh and that they are black people like him. Then they separate from one another and take different paths, embarking on a new stage in a long journey. These bones symbolize African slaves, Loomis's ancestors who perished in the holds of slaveships and whose bodies were tossed into the Atlantic Ocean; dead Africans who never made it physically across the water but are an integral part of the whole black experience in America. Unwilling pioneers in a massive racial struggle for survival, they were the first victims of a terrible odyssey. For two centuries their memory was part of an important link between the old African tradition and an emerging African-American identity.

To understand his true identity and his destiny in this country, Loomis must relive the whole experience of his race. Having already endured slavery, he now returns to the moment when his people arrived at these shores, for his spirit must make the journey from the beginning. As the dead rise from the ocean, join the survivors on the shore, and a whole race of forgotten people wend their way across the new land, Loomis knows he must reconnect with his African forebears, for they are survivors and they alone can free his African spirit. The path to spiritual and physical liberty lies in a reunion with the past, and, once his spirit merges with the spirits of his African ancestors, the momentum of that great migration will sweep him to freedom. But, try as he may, he cannot rise to join his ancestors. The door to salvation lies open, but he does not yet have the strength to walk through, to be united with the past, and to find his true place in this land. The ordeal continues.

As Loomis, overcome by the apparition, lies on the floor as exhausted as the bodies of his ancestors on the seashore, Bynum helps him articulate the dream, for he had a similar revelation when he met the spirit of his father. Like a preacher and his congregation elucidating a passage of Scripture, the two of them explore the text of the vision. Their sing-song call and response as they complete each other's thoughts, repeating words and phrases, recalls the rhythmic structure of black church ceremonies and the basic pattern of the blues, which, in turn, is reminiscent of African music.[9] Thus, this journey of revelation through a racial consciousness bears the unmistakable mark of an African-American spirituality.[10]

According to Stuckey, the ring shouts and juba dance—which occur at the beginning of this scene—were important features of African ancestral ceremonies: "They gathered on the principal occasions of worship, above all at ancestral ceremonies, the most important of which in North America was the ring shout, which often was but one aspect, however important, of multifaceted African religious observance" (16). How the ring shouts led to spirit possession is described by Marshall Stearns:

> The dancers form a circle in the center of the floor, one in back of another. Then they begin to shuffle in a counter-clockwise direction around and around, arms out and shoulders hunched. A fantastic rhythm is built up by the rest of the group standing back to the walls, who clap their hands and stomp on the floor. . . . Suddenly sisters and brothers scream and spin, possessed by religious hysteria, like corn starting to pop over a hot fire. . . . This is actually a West African circle dance . . . a complicated and sacred ritual. (12–13)

Although Loomis's African identity makes strong claims on him, the Holy Ghost still holds him in thrall by keeping his wife from him. Trapped in the confusing twilight between these two traditions, he is unable to determine which of them will enslave him and which will set him free. The answer to that will come the moment he discovers his precise identity, for, as Bynum says, he is still a man "who done forgot his song." Like the caged bird that does not sing, an enslaved man loses contact with his identity, which must be rediscovered when freedom is restored. Loomis must purge his tormented spirit of the brutal effects of slavery. Joe Turner owned him for seven years, crushed his spirit, and tried to possess him, just as slave owners of the past had tried to turn their captives into chattel. Loomis is one of the lucky ones—he was released before he lost complete hold on his identity, before Joe Turner captured it for good. But he has forgotten what it is like to be free, and his perception of his real self is buried deep in his subconscious, trapped under the debris of a tortured spirit. Indeed, the old Christian Loomis is lost forever and is being replaced by the emergence of a more ancient African Loomis. But he needs to dredge the depths of his soul to release this identity. He must learn to sing his true song. Alienated from himself, he has to do what Bynum did: recognize and restructure all the fragments and characteristics from his life and racial memory that have molded him into a unique human being.

> BYNUM: It was my song. It had come from deep inside me. I looked back in memory and gathered up pieces and snatches of things to make that song. I was making it up out of myself. . . . It got so I used up all of myself in the making of that song. (71)

Finding his song means starting a new life of freedom. He must examine all the forces that shaped and set him on the path that led to a chain gang. While this involves a reunion with the distant past of his ancestors, it also means seeking a reconciliation with the immediate past in the person of his wife. He thinks his wife will provide a beginning, that she will rescue him from the strange world he has been traversing and help him forge a new world to fit his needs, a world with enough room for him and his song. All he needs, he thinks, is a starting point. But Mattie Campbell knows there is none— or rather, every point is a potential starting place. There are no ready-made niches waiting for black people; they have to carve their own with the materials at hand.

In some ways, Mattie and Loomis are kindred spirits embarked on similar pilgrimages. Mattie's search for her husband has become, under Bynum's gentle prodding, a search for a man who, in Bertha's words, has "some understanding and [is] willing to work with that understanding to come to the best he can." In other words, not a man like Jeremy who needed to go out and garner some more life experiences, but a man who has discovered himself. Loomis, on his part, is searching for his wife, but he sees in Mattie someone who could fill the empty spaces in his life. As each of them gropes toward a new identity they appear to be headed in the same direction. But they must first take that final step toward self-empowerment; they have to affirm their individual identities separately before beginning a journey together:

LOOMIS: Come here and let me touch you. I been watching you. You a full woman. A man needs a full woman. Come and be with me.

MATTIE: I ain't got enough for you. You'd use me up too fast.

LOOMIS: (He goes to touch her but finds he cannot.) I done forgot how to touch.

The tension at the inn grows to a feverish pitch as the religious battle within Loomis assumes cosmic proportions. Reflecting this combat, the very forces of nature appear to be in turmoil, concentrated on this household. The two children, Zonia and Reuben, sense the sharpening tone as Bynum's chanting in the yard sounds like a conversation with the wind that grows louder and more fierce. Reuben claims that the ghost of Seth's mother appeared to him to chide him for not releasing his pigeons as he had promised his dead friend Eugene.[11] This flurry of nocturnal activity foreshadows the events of the final scene when Loomis finally confronts his wife, Martha. Almost as soon as they meet, it is obvious that their lives have taken divergent routes. After waiting years for her husband to return, Martha was forced to give him up for dead. The Evangelist church helped her pick up the pieces of her life, and she owes it allegiance. Loomis realizes that their lives are different now, that there is no compelling bond between them anymore. In that moment he understands why he was searching for her—not to be reunited, but to say goodbye to her and close the book on his earlier life:

> I been waiting to look on your face to say my goodbye. That goodbye got so big at times, it seem like it was gonna swallow me up. Like Jonah in the whale's belly I sat in that goodbye for three years. That goodbye kept me out on the road searching. Not looking on women in their houses. It kept me bound up to the road. All the time that goodbye swelling up in my chest till I'm about to bust. Now that I can see your face I can say my goodbye and make my own world. (90)

The goodbye is also a reconciliation. After ten years they know their separation was not of their own making; they were victims of

circumstance. This reunion thus becomes the moment of a new separation that will lead to full self-affirmation. For Martha, it is the
culmination of her search—she makes peace with her husband and
is reunited with her daughter. Aware that Loomis and Martha were
headed in different spiritual directions, Bynum bound Zonia to her
mother, forcing Loomis to continue searching for his wife. Of course,
Loomis and Martha cannot completely sever the bonds between
them, for as long as Zonia is alive they will always be united in her.

Once he has returned his daughter to her mother and said goodbye to his wife, Loomis enters the final stage of his quest—self-empowerment in the full realization of his true cultural identity. All his
life he has been restrained from pursuing his own destiny: "Everywhere I go people wanna bind me up. Joe Turner wanna bind me up!
Reverend Toliver wanna bind me up. You wanna bind me up. Well,
Joe Turner's come and gone and Herald Loomis ain't for no binding. I ain't gonna let nobody bind me up!" (91). Now he is ready to
break free of the psychological and spiritual bonds that hold him.
Martha exhorts him to be faithful to the Christian tenets, to embrace
Christianity once again: "Even if you done fell away from the church
you can be saved again." But, in Loomis's mind, it is the church, not
he, that has sinned. Christianity is at the root of many of his problems and the problems of his people. White Christian men sold black
Africans into slavery and the white God, Jesus Christ, in whose name
and under whose protective banner plantation owners exploited their
cotton-picking slaves, blessed his white disciples for their efforts:

> And all I seen was a bunch of niggers dazed out of their woolly
> heads. And Mr. Jesus Christ standing there in the middle of them,
> grinning. . . . He grin that big old grin . . . and niggers wallowing
> at his feet. . . . Great big old white man . . . your Mr. Jesus Christ.
> Standing there with a whip in one hand and tote board in anoth-
> er, and them niggers swimming in a sea of cotton. And he count-
> ing. He tallying up the cotton. "Well, Jeremiah . . . what's the
> matter, you ain't picked but two hundred pounds of cotton today?
> Got to put you on half rations." And Jeremiah go back and lay
> up there on his half rations and talk about what a nice man Mr.
> Jesus Christ is 'cause he give him salvation after he die. Something
> wrong here. Something don't fit right! (93)

Christianity engendered in black slaves a passive resignation toward their fate. When the promise of salvation in the next world was offered as the panacea to all their problems in this one, it created in them a proclivity for suffering, enabling the white man to continue his subjugation of them. In his book *Foundations of Christianity,* Karl Kautsky argues that ancient slaves obeyed their masters out of fear, whereas Christianity raised the spineless obedience of slaves to a moral duty incumbent even upon free men (355–56).

Like Levee in *Ma Rainey,* Loomis directs his anger against a Christianity that stood by while black men and women were brutalized, the Christianity in whose service he was laboring when Joe Turner kidnapped him. Many atrocities during slavery were committed in the name of Christianity by owners who believed that their Christian upbringing endowed them with the moral authority to enslave African "savages."[12] Hence Loomis's image of Jesus Christ as an overseer. In *Roll, Jordan, Roll,* Genovese discusses Nietzsche's description of this aspect of Christianity as a weapon of subjugation:[13]

> The notion of Christianity as a religion of slaves rose long before Nietzsche's polemics, which nonetheless must be credited with imparting to it special force and clarity. "The Christian faith, from the beginning," Nietzsche insists, "is sacrifice: the sacrifice of all freedom, all pride, all self-confidence of spirit; it is at the same time subjection, self-derision, and self-mutilation." This cruel religion of painful subjection, he continues, softened the slaves by drawing hatred from their souls, and without hatred there could be no revolt. (162–63)

Loomis now knows that Christianity has never brought him relief from suffering, that the pledge of salvation is no balm for the pain: "I been wading in the water. I been walking all over the River Jordan. But what it get me, huh? I done been baptized with blood of the lamb and the fire of the Holy Ghost. But what I got, huh? I got salvation? My enemies all around me picking the flesh from my bones. I'm choking on my own blood and all you got to give me is salvation?" (93). He needs the freedom of this life, not the rewards of the next. That freedom can come only from a realization that he truly belongs to himself—not to Joe Turner, not to

Jesus Christ, but to Herald Loomis, former African slave and re-vitalized African American.

The Christian tradition finds its salvation in the suffering scape-goat figure of Christ the sacrificial lamb. Loomis does not need such a figure, for he has done his own suffering: "I don't need nobody to bleed for me! I can bleed for myself." The realization that the shed-ding of his own blood is both baptism and resurrection sweeps over him with a transcendental force that finally sets his spirit free. As he slashes himself across the chest and rubs his cleansing blood over his face, the conflict within him reaches its apogee and the African emerg-es free. Paul Carter Harrison's suggestion that this blood-letting is a reenactment of the "Osirian mythos, which invites the death of the body in order to allow for the resurrection of the spirit/body" (313), locates this ritual firmly within the African cosmology. Sterling Stuck-ey's parallel between the black Christian preacher and the African priest suggests Loomis's spiritual African ancestry long before Joe Turner captured him: "One errs in assuming that the slave preacher was primarily Christian and did not play a variety of religious roles, especially that of African priest. . . . The preacher's priestly or Afri-can function . . . was guarded from whites. . . . Therefore, if the Af-rican religious leader was to operate in the open, the safest cloak to hide behind was that of Christianity" (38). This moment of realiza-tion is therefore not an isolated event but the culmination of a sub-liminal process that gathered force from all the experiences of Loo-mis's past. It is at once a divestiture of his Christian identity and a full embrace of his true identity as an African, free in the land that was once his dungeon. Now he can stand up straight, for his knees are no longer bent in servitude. He has found his song, banished the hellhounds chasing him, and can join the spirits of his ancestors as they march to freedom. Having witnessed his self-empowerment, Mattie Campbell now knows they can make room in their lives for each other, and she runs after him as he walks away.

Bynum recognizes the blood-cleansing as a reenactment of his shiny man's ritual, and, as Loomis runs from the room, Bynum knows that his own search has also ended. He has found his shiny man: "Her-ald Loomis, you shining! You shining like new money!" Loomis's name, Herald, suits the title of the shiny man—One Who Goes Before and Shows the Way. But he is no harbinger of Christianity like John the Baptist. Instead, he ushers in a new tradition. His experiences demonstrate that the path to the true destinies of black people begins in their African roots: only when they embrace their African identities completely will they really be free. This journey is extremely painful, involving, on some level, reliving the agonies of the past, for the road to Africa must pass through the plantations of slavery. Wilson seems to be saying that slavery is an unalterable fact of black history, forever etched in the consciousness of black people. Ignoring it will cause it to fester. Only by facing it with fortitude and by celebrating their release will blacks achieve its purgation.[14] That done, they can face freedom as survivors and claim that slavery, like Joe Turner, has come and gone.

The conflict between Christian and African identities reaches a different resolution in each character. They reside harmoniously in Bertha, providing her with a broad base to define her actions and her self. In Bynum, the African flourishes, but there are traces of Christianity in his apocalyptic experiences. Herald Loomis wars with and rejects Christianity in favor of his "African-ness." In him, Wilson has created a character who is at once a sharply drawn individual and an allegorical figure. His life encapsulates and parallels the entire black experience: stolen and enslaved, forced to work on a cotton plantation, freed, separated from his family, reunited physically with his immediate past and spiritually with his distant past.

In the gradual replacement of Christian ceremony with African ritual a significant development occurs. Herald Loomis slowly replaces Jesus Christ. Like Christ, he is the sacrificial scapegoat whose suffering opens the door to salvation. Like Christ, he points the way to a new identity and a new life, a way that will not be so painful now that he and others like him have shouldered the burden of suffering. And if Bynum's first shiny man was like John the Baptist, the one to follow would have to be like Christ. Just as Christ rounded off the work begun by John, so Loomis sets the final seal of approval on Bynum's work. And finally, by rejecting Christ's blood in favor of his own, Loomis completes the substitution.

Further clues to this development lie in Loomis's visionary experience with the march of the bones, a moment replete with shamanistic dimensions. In *Shamanism: Archaic Techniques of Ecstasy*, Mircea Eliade writes that

> the shaman's instruction often takes place in dreams. It is in dreams that the pure sacred life is entered and direct relations with the gods, spirits, and ancestral souls are re-established. It is always in dreams that historical time is abolished and mythical time regained—which allows the future shaman to witness the beginnings of the world and hence to become contemporary not only with the cosmogony but also with the primordial mythical revelations. (103)

Loomis visits the souls of his ancestors, witnesses the genesis of the African-American experience, and, from the dead, obtains clues to his cultural identity and direction for his future. Through his contact with those spirits he becomes privy to secrets that lie beyond the reach of the living. "'Seeing Spirits,' in dream or awake," Eliade contends, "is the determining sign of the shamanic vocation, whether spontaneous or voluntary. For, in a manner, having contact with the souls of the dead signifies *being dead oneself* . . . for the dead know everything" (84). Eliade also suggests that "shamanic initiation . . . sometimes preserves the perfect schema of a ritual death and resurrection." Christ's death and resurrection are often seen as his passage to and from the land of the dead. The element of ritual death is present in Loomis's visionary experience, only the resurrection is delayed a while longer. When added to the other signs, this reinforces the image of Loomis as a kind of Christ-figure. But there is a dual complexity in Loomis's apotheosis, for his blood-letting and shamanic visitations bear traces of both Christian and Osirian mythology.

Herald Loomis's quest for self-empowerment has thus taken him on a spiritual journey to his ancient cultural roots. At the start of the play he has already traveled most of the way, but then, needing help over the last hurdle, his steps lead him to Seth Holly's inn where Bynum awaits him. In this house of transition, which seems to stand at the confluence of many roads and where other wandering black folk discover new paths toward their own destinies, the conjurer and the ex-slave make their shamanistic voyage toward knowledge and self-fulfillment. On a more mundane plane, Loomis finds his wife and thus ensures a safe haven for his daughter.

Old journeys end and new, profitable ones begin for all the characters—Martha and Zonia are reunited, Jeremy and Molly find each other, Mattie now has a chance to experience fulfillment with a newly empowered Loomis, Bynum receives the seal of approval on the work that he will continue to perform, and the Holly inn remains the prism through which confused and tired men and women can find their dark journeys transformed by light and new direction.

This play is an Afro-Christian tapestry woven with threads from both traditions. In various ways the characters seek self-affirmation through constant spiritual renegotiations between the symbols and customs of African and Christian mythology. Their road to self-fulfillment begins by reconnecting themselves with their past through music and rituals. This reunion provides them with a proper perspective of their tumultuous history, as they discover their true origins not in the plantations of slavery but in the rich and varied cultures of Africa, though the South has played a part in shaping their destinies. They discover their real identities to be African, not Christian, though this "African-ness" is transfigured with multiple images drawn from a Christianity in which they may find truth and affirmation of their deepest beliefs.

4

THE PIANO LESSON

FROM DISCORD TO HARMONY

In 1936, the Organization of the National Negro Congress was founded. In bringing together more than five hundred black organizations, it marked the first real attempt by blacks to establish a consolidated national presence. By the mid-thirties, blacks had begun to settle in various cities in the northern United States. The two previous decades had witnessed the height of the migration from the South; by now, the flow of blacks into northern towns had stabilized. The swing and big band era had hit its stride, and such artists as Louis Armstrong, Count Basie, and Duke Ellington were fast becoming household names. The cultural identity of black Americans was being defined by jazz, which, over the next few decades, would influence and shape the culture of the entire country. Before the end of the half-century, American music would be synonymous with jazz.

The thirties were the decade in which black music and black performers made the greatest progress toward national recognition, not only in jazz, but also in classical and folk music. The year 1931 saw the first performance by a major orchestra of a black composer's symphony when William Grant Still's *Afro-American Symphony* was performed by the Rochester (New York) Philharmonic Symphony Orchestra. In 1932, Thomas Andrew Dorsey founded the National Convention of Gospel Choirs and Choruses in Chicago. In 1933, the first Negro folk opera written by a black composer was performed on Broadway—*Run Little Chillun* by Hall Johnson. And throughout the decade black-authored musicals continued to be produced on stage in New York: *Hot Chocolates* (at the Hudson Theatre, 1929–30), *Change Your Luck* (at the George N. Cohen Theatre, 1930), *Sugar Hill* (at the Forrest Theatre, 1931), *Black Rhythm* (at the Comedy Theatre, 1936), *Swing It* (at the Adelphi Theatre, 1937), and *Brownskin Models* (a series of annual revues, begun in 1925, which continued to be produced throughout the 1930s).[1] In 1930, Willis Richardson edited his first anthology of black plays, *Plays and Pageants from the Life of the Negro,* and in 1935, he published his second anthology, *Negro History in Thirteen Plays.* Also produced in the 1930s were several plays by such playwrights as Richardson, Randolph Edmonds, and Langston Hughes; the prominent black theater companies were the Krigwa Players (1926), Harlem Experimental Theatre (1928), Harlem Suitcase Theatre (1937), and Rose McClendon Players (1938); and the Federal Theatre Project, started in 1935, provided work for black actors, playwrights, singers, and dancers.

Despite this recognition of black artists, black people were still embroiled in a fight for survival. They continued to be treated like leftovers of history, dregs in the great melting pot of America. Musicians like Duke Ellington performed for all-white audiences at such places as the Cotton Club in Harlem, an ironic reminder of slavery when blacks fiddled while their masters danced. Then there was the Depression, difficult enough for most Americans but devastating for blacks who were hard-pressed to find jobs even in normal circumstances. By the middle of the decade, however, the national economic scene had begun to stabilize. It is in this time, in 1936, that Wilson sets *The Piano Lesson.*

In the three earlier plays,[2] migration to the North is a major theme, with characters traveling long journeys in search of jobs, relationships, and self-affirmation. In *The Piano Lesson,* we are introduced to characters eager to return to the South. This is significant, for it marks a potential turning point in the fortunes of black people. Up to now, their search for their true identities—while ending in Africa—had been accompanied by journeys to the North, away from their farms and families. For the first time a character suggests the South as a place for them to pursue their destinies as free men and women.

The search for self-authentication continues in *The Piano Lesson,* where Wilson finds new meaning in the same themes of separation, migration, and reunion. As in *Fences,* separation occurs on a psychological level in a rift between a brother and sister grappling with their memories, their debts to the past, and their emerging roles as free blacks in an antagonistic society. Migration and the pros and cons of staying south or going north—issues hinted at in *Joe Turner* and implicit in the sorry plight of urban blacks in *Ma Rainey* and *Fences*—are given new voice by the characters in this play. And reunion and reconciliation with the past continue to heal the wounds of the present, bridge chasms between loved ones, and clear the air for a creative future.

By 1936, several thousand blacks had settled in the northern industrial belt, hacking out their own version of freedom, grasping for the American dream but living an American nightmare of poverty and discrimination in a capitalist society. Years of thwarted hopes and unfulfilled ambitions had filled them with a desperation that would simmer for a few more decades before exploding into violence during the latter part of the century. The lives of many of the characters in *The Piano Lesson* exemplify this despair.

This play is the story of the Charles family and its efforts to exorcize the ghosts that haunt it. Berniece and her brother, Boy Willie, fight over a piano in her house in Pittsburgh—he wants to sell it and she wants it left there. The play's setting describes the Charles household as lacking "warmth and vigor," and Berniece's air of mourning adds a tone of gloom to the atmosphere. Unable to come to terms with the death of her husband, Crawley, three years ago, she clings to the memories of a tragic past. She greets her brother's arrival with suspicion, accuses him and and his friend, Lymon, of stealing the truck in which they drove north, and ungraciously tells them to be on their way quickly. When Sutter's ghost appears to her and calls for Boy Willie, she immediately assumes that he has murdered Sutter. All this sets an uneasy stage for the conflict to come.

In Wilson's plays, the blues is the seam that threads the themes together. It also casts an emotional aura over the characters, uniting a group of seemingly diverse personalities with a bond forged in a common past. The fascinating complex of this music is that although it keeps alive "the painful details and episodes of a brutal experience" (Ellison 78), in one magnificent leap it elevates black people from the status of slaves to the level of artists. Something so compelling quickly became a commercial prospect in the burgeoning bazaar of twentieth-century urban America and, therefore, a source of great power to performers like Ma Rainey. Small wonder then that even as this music provided blacks with a passport to a world beyond the plantation, it also became a threat to the white people who controlled that world; and they moved quickly to bridle its galloping pace. In *Joe Turner,* the music-makers at Seefus's bar were "liable to end up in a raid and go to jail sure enough"; Ma Rainey complained that white people "take [her] voice and trap it in them fancy boxes with all them buttons and dials"; and Levee's songs were belittled and snatched up for a paltry five dollars apiece. In *The Piano Lesson,* Wining Boy is driven almost to desperation by the attempts to suck the music from him:

> Go to a place and they find out you play piano, the first thing they want to do is give you a drink, find you a piano and sit you right down.... They ain't gonna let you get up! ... You look up one day... and you hate the piano. But that's all you got. You can't do nothing else. All you know to do is play that piano. Now, who am I? Am I me ... or am I the piano player? Sometimes it seem like the only thing to do is shoot the piano player cause he's the cause of all the trouble I'm having. (41)

The music that defined blacks and became inextricably merged with their cultural identity has now placed them in jeopardy. It has given them a renewed sense of themselves as well as a new vulnerability. Sensing the power of this music for which blacks will go to jail, white folks want to own it. In *Joe Turner,* Bynum perceived the deeper significance of Joe Turner's actions: "What he wanted was your song. He wanted to have that song to be his. He thought by catching you he could learn that song. Every nigger he catch he's looking for the one he can learn that song from" (*Joe Turner* 73). In 1911, Joe Turner had kidnapped black people into slavery in order to "possess their song." In 1936, a white man is still trying to capture their song; this time, by buying the instruments that produce it—there are several references in the play to a mysterious white man who is "going around to all the colored people's houses looking to buy up musical instruments." The process of trying to rob the black man of the source of his identity—and his power—continues. The music that gave meaning to his freedom could force him into a different kind of slavery, for even as it soothes it creates a new dilemma.

In her essay "The Songs of a Marked Man," Margaret E. Glover writes of this predicament: "His music gave the black man a place in the white man's world, but at the cost of losing his right to that music and the part of himself he put in it" (69). For blacks at this point in their history, the only avenue into mainstream America was through their music.[3] It was their only bargaining chip at the table of integration. But they ran the risk of losing possession of it, and with it their hard-earned identity. One aspect of the dilemma that *The Piano Lesson* addresses is that, by clinging to their past and their identity as a separate people, blacks are doomed to be onlookers rather than participants in the bounty of their country; yet any attempt to enter the mainstream could compromise this identity.

This quandary is given physical shape through the use of a central symbol—the piano, which used to be in the Sutter household and now stands in the center of the Charles house. As a piano in a black household, its obvious symbolism refers to the blues. But this particular instrument has a more potent signification: it has played a pivotal role in the fight for freedom, and its very presence in this household is an eloquent testament to the success of that effort. Its history is a direct reflection of the struggle that engendered the blues. The masklike images on it are superbly rendered in the style of African sculpture, which elevates them above mere craftsmanship into an artistic dimension. Recording the history of this family for several generations—portraits, weddings, funerals, and other events, including slave sales—they imbue the piano with a totemic aura, for it now symbolizes the struggle of one family to survive slavery and sharecropping. The power of art to transcend the restraining barriers of time and space is dramatically portrayed in the way these images have kept together a dispersed family. As it stands in this household, the piano seems to possess a mystical power that keeps alive the spirits of the dead, encouraging a communion between past and present.

The piano also has the potential to reflect the personalities of those who come into contact with it. Every living member of this family reacts differently to it, according to his or her past actions, hopes, fears, and desires. It thus becomes a touchstone to evaluate their attitudes and dispositions. To Berniece—whose life has been spent in the shadow of violence and death—it is a millstone round her neck, trapping her in a vortex of painful memories, dragging her into the depths of a past she wants to forget. First her father, Boy Charles, was burnt to death. Then her husband died in a shootout with the sheriff during a wood-stealing foray with Boy Willie and Lymon. Between these two incidents were long, hard years as the fatherless family struggled to survive. The piano is a powerful reminder of all this. She cannot bring herself to play it, afraid to release a torrent of pent-up emotions. Yet she will not part with this repository of her family's pain. To be rid of it might purge that suffering, but it would also sever the only link with her ancestors. As Mei-Ling Ching writes in her essay "Two Notes on August Wilson," to Berniece "the piano is both a legacy and a taboo" (71). It is a sacred relic of her past, a reminder of the misery her family endured; by keeping it she pays homage to their sacrifices. But she also keeps alive the anguish associated with that past. Giving it up might relieve some of her pain but not without betraying her deepest roots, an action that contains its own pain. There is, therefore, a kind of desperation in her refusal to let Boy Willie sell it. Her distress is evident as she lashes out against the very people whose memory she holds dear, blaming her father for getting killed and leaving her mother alone for seventeen years.

So her memories fester, and the piano stands there, untouched by her. Once, she played for her mother who sought to keep the past alive through the piano. But the day her mother died she stopped playing it, unwilling to stay tied to the past the way the older woman had been. Ironically, by not playing the piano, Berniece allows her wounds to remain tender. Avery knows that her only chance to be free is through the music; by rejecting it she remains enslaved to the past. Sensing the power of the piano to release her spirit from bondage, he exhorts her to play: "You can walk over there right now and play that piano. You can walk over there right now and God will walk over there with you. . . . Come on play 'Old Ship of Zion.' Walk over here and claim it as an instrument of the Lord. You can walk over here right now and make it into a celebration" (70). But Berniece cannot do it. The pain is still too raw. For now, the past has too powerful a hold on her, and she must find a way to break free and discover her true self. Her scene with Lymon—a remarkable love-duet of mixed signals, yearning, and tenderness—is evidence of her deep frustrations, her love-starved spirit, and her inability to release herself to her desires.

On the one hand, Berniece's grief is real and deep, for it has not been easy growing up without a father, then losing a husband and being forced to raise a little girl by herself. On the other hand, her three years of mourning contain not a little self-pity as she draws her grief around her like a neurotic cloak, taking shelter from life and the world. Indulging in her memories anesthetizes her aching spirit, enveloping her with a protective numbness. By clinging to the past she does not have to face the challenges of the present and the future; she can retreat into the false security of her denials. The sham of this security is exposed when Boy Willie threatens to take away its symbol—the piano. As her cocoon of grief is shattered, the old wounds are reopened, and frustration and anger gush forth as she wildly accuses her brother of killing her husband.

Avery manages to sidestep the crossfire between Berniece and Boy Willie. An enterprising young man, he has worked hard to put his past behind him and make a successful life for himself in Pittsburgh. Very much at home in the big city, he has found "opportunities for growth and advancement that did not exist for him in the rural South." Working as an elevator attendant in a downtown building, he has ambitious plans to start his own church. A self-styled preacher, he claims to have been called by God to lead black people to a better, safer life. But there is a sycophantic side to him that Boy Willie remembers: "Avery think all white men is bigshots. He don't know there some white men ain't got as much as he got" (11).

Like Levee, Avery faces the dilemma of deciding how much of himself he can compromise without "selling out" to the white man. Levee needed to court Sturdyvant to get a recording contract. To this end he compromised his music and his cultural identity, which resulted in alienation from his own people and spiritual havoc. Avery takes the small favors—half a day off to go to the bank, a turkey for Thanksgiving—because he has set his sights on greater things: to be a leader among his own people. His delicate balancing act between these two societies is evident when he sends a white man to buy the piano from Berniece and then, realizing how much it means to her, supports her decision to keep it. Indeed, he even forgets the name of the would-be buyer. Now he wants Berniece to use the piano in the service of the Lord and to release her spirit from the captivity of grief.

Avery's search for self-empowerment leads him to walk a fine line between both races. While he does kowtow to the white man, thereby incurring the mild disdain of Boy Willie, he means well and is genuinely concerned for the welfare of his people. Although he and Levee face a similar dilemma, their responses are different because their backgrounds are different. Levee's horrible experiences made him abrasive and eventually destroyed him. Avery is honest, intelligent, and compliant. While there may be more than a tinge of vainglory in the way he packages himself as a spiritual leader of his people, he is basically a caring black man struggling to survive as best he can in a white world. His donning of the preacher's mantle is part of a continuing African tradition. As Stuckey suggests, "the old Negro preacher and other religious leaders in the slave community were the ones who spoke for their people whatever their ethnic origins. The authority of major religious leaders on the plantations owed much to the divine-kingship systems of West Africa and for that reason was the least likely to be questioned" (38). In this role, Avery is responding to a call from his cultural past that came to him in a dream, the racial conduit between past and present.

In sharp contrast to the solid—almost stolid—Avery is Wining Boy, uncle to Boy Willie and Berniece. A musician and gambler, he was probably similar to the spirited Jeremy Furlow (from *Joe Turner*) before twenty-five years of roaming from town to town and bar to bar finally blunted his sense of adventure. In *Joe Turner,* Wilson examines the reasons that propelled blacks on peripatetic journeys throughout America. Wining Boy used to be one of those restless bluesmen searching for spiritual fulfillment. Now, years later, he is ready to go home.

When he left the South, Wining Boy took with him little more than the blues. It was his companion, keeping him on the move and bringing him luck at the gambling tables. As long as it was with him he had a sackful of money and the desire to travel. Throughout his journeys he drew strength from the blues and the knowledge that his wife would always have a home waiting for him. But slowly the music became a burden. Wherever he went people forced him to play, tying him to a piano for hours at a stretch. What started as a spontaneous impulse became an imposition, and gradually he began to reject the music, to "hate the piano" and distance himself emotionally from the very thing that defined him. Now his wife is dead and he has lost touch with the blues. Spiritually bereft, he seeks renewal in a reunion with his roots in the South.[4] After years of searching, he realizes that his home is exactly where it had always been—the place he left all those years ago.

Although the blues finds its origins in the music of Africa, it is essentially an American creation, fired in the kiln of slavery and honed on the anvil of the post-Reconstruction era. In *Joe Turner,* an ex-slave reaches into his African past for confirmation of self-worth; twenty-five years later, in *The Piano Lesson,* an ex-bluesman is returning to his African-American past in search of his lost self. The difference in perception is enormous. In the 1911 of *Joe Turner,* when the blues was in an embryonic stage, black Americans, still smarting from the scars of slavery and the broken promises of Reconstruction, had to look back three hundred years for clues to their cultural identity. In *The Piano Lesson,* some of those clues can be found in the South. By 1936, the blues had made the transition from a folk music to an art form. In it, blacks had found a touchstone to measure their cultural worth; they now had something they could call their own. Moreover, the blues and jazz were becoming America's music; they were beginning to define the culture of the whole nation. With this realization and the healing distance of time came a new perception of the South. More than just the home of slavery, it was now also the birthplace of the blues, the soil in which their new roots—as African Americans—were embedded.

This play depicts a growing realization by blacks that they can call the South their home, because several generations of their families grew up there and paid a great price on the plantations that built the South.[5] Besides, they have discovered that the North is not as rosy as it once looked. The lives of all the Wilson characters in *Joe Turner, Ma Rainey,* and *The Piano Lesson* bear witness to Northern racism. The "good jobs" available are running elevators (*Piano Lesson* 23). Not till the end of *Fences,* in 1965, will things turn for the better. Long before that, in *The Piano Lesson,* blacks are beginning to look again at what they left behind. After twenty-five years of wandering, during which time his wife died and he found himself alienated from his music, Wining Boy has realized that his real home is the South, for his emotional roots are buried there.

But the desire to return home does not guarantee a warm welcome. While the South may be a nostalgic salve for spirits bruised by the indifference and hostility of the North, the possibilities of a productive life there are minimal. A century of industrialization has focused the industry and enterprise of America on northern urban growth, and the rural South is no longer the land of plenty it once was. With the failure of the stock market forcing cotton plantations into desuetude, the South, which never really recovered from the effects of the Civil War, has become an even greater economic disaster. According to Doaker, the only reason why blacks are allowed to buy land there is that it is worthless. Then there is the question of ownership. Wining Boy points out that even if a black man did buy land in the South, for all practical purposes it would still belong to the white man, who has the law on his side. The harsh truth is clear: there is no place where blacks will be received gladly—not yet, anyway.

Lymon, however, does not know this. To him the North holds the answer to all his problems. In the South he lived in the shadow of a law that found creative ways to keep him enslaved to the white man: "Fined me a hundred dollars. Mr. Stovall come and paid my hundred dollars and the judge say I got to work for him to pay back his hundred dollars. I told him I'd rather take my thirty days but they wouldn't do that" (37). He is full of enthusiasm about his prospects in the North, sure that he will get a job and a girl. He even buys Wining Boy's suit in the hope that it will help him find a girl. In a visual exchange charged with significance, Wining Boy gives up the suit—almost as if he is shedding his urban demeanor—as he prepares to go back to the rural South, and Lymon puts it on to face life in the urban North. The contrast is poignant: the older man, jaded and spent, searching for his lost self through a spiritual renewal with his roots; and the youth, starry-eyed and buoyant, leaving his roots to carve a new future for himself.

There is also a significant contrast in attitude between Lymon and Boy Willie. Close friends, they came north together, but with vastly different visions of themselves as black men. Lymon will use his share of the money from the watermelons to tide him over as he joins the mass of hopeful black people scrambling for jobs and a better life in an environment they barely understand. Boy Willie will take his share of the money from the sale of the fruit and the piano and go back south. It is no wonder that they part company when they are on the verge of getting what they came for—just as Boy Willie is poised to take the piano, Lymon leaves him to go after Grace. Perhaps Lymon will have better luck than most people; after all, he does get his girl by the end of the play. Or perhaps the experiences of the other characters suggest that he will end up either drained of all his enthusiasm, like Wining Boy, or bitter, like Berniece. Without the docile attitude that Avery used to his advantage, Lymon's material success is doubtful, for this white society clips the wings of energetic black men and rewards the submissive ones. Wilson makes obvious this dissimilarity between Avery and Lymon when Lymon says he would love to fly a plane (he seeks the heady rush of true freedom) but is afraid of an elevator (symbolic of a cage), whereas Avery prefers the humdrum rhythm of an elevator secured by steel cables to the soaring joy of an airplane ride.

Doaker manifests no yearning for the South. Quite happy with his current lifestyle as a railroad cook, he gives the impression of having lived through so much that nothing now could disconcert him. His imperturbable demeanor derives from his twenty-seven years with the railroad, half a lifetime of traveling that has calmed much of his restlessness, although he does continue in his job. His sense of balance and rhythm is absent in the other characters, and he appears to be at peace with himself. In that, he bears some resemblance to Bynum in *Joe Turner,* Slow Drag in *Ma Rainey,* and even Bono in *Fences.* Not without emotion, they walk the middle line wonderfully; wise, experienced, and mature, they have developed a strong sense of who they are and what their roles might be. Without ignoring Boy Willie and Berniece, Doaker avoids taking sides in their battle. Indeed, he displays a subtle compassion for both their positions. He seems intuitively to understand their needs, to realize that ultimately they both seek the same thing—reconciliation with their past. Having lived through so much strife, he wants peace among his relatives. Although Doaker had helped his brother take the piano from Sutter's house, he now considers it the cause of too much suffering and would rather Berniece got rid of it. This family has lost many members because of it, and, with Sutter's ghost on the prowl, he knows there could be problems ahead. Toward the end of the play, as Sutter's presence in their house gets stronger, Doaker blames the piano for all their trouble and tells Avery to bless it.

Doaker presides over this house as an elder statesman, defusing angry outbursts, offering sage words of advice, and keeping the conflict between brother and sister under control until fate and the supernatural elements take a hand and the conflict reaches a profound, almost mystical level, beyond argument and reason. In *Joe Turner,* Bertha, with her nurturing ways and calming presence, has a similar function to that of Doaker. Both of them maintain the balance of a household threatening to go awry. It is significant that Doaker also is a cook and that this play, like *Joe Turner,* also takes place mainly in a kitchen, perhaps the most important room in a black household. Even during slavery, the kitchen was the only place where a slave held some sway. Eugene Genovese suggests that white cuisine derived from the art of the black cook: "The high praise of southern cooking . . . has usually been lavished on Ole Missus. . . . The truth is that Ole

Mammy, or merely 'the cook,' usually ran the kitchen with an iron hand and had learned what she knew from generations of black predecessors. What Missus knew, she usually learned from her cook, not vice versa" (540–41). Thus, the seat of power traditionally resided in the kitchen, and whoever ruled the roast ran the household—Bertha in *Joe Turner* and Doaker in *The Piano Lesson*.[6]

Doaker is a survivor. He lives in the present, not in the past like his brother did. It means viewing the world as rationally as he can, without letting sentimentality cloud his vision of goals that are already very hard to achieve. For years, he watched as black people ran heedlessly into trouble. With the railroad he had a ringside seat at the traveling circus of blacks desperate to get away from their plight, plunging headlong into disaster; there he witnessed, firsthand, their naïveté and the futility of their journeys: "I wish I had a dollar for every time that someone wasn't at the station to meet them. I done seen that a lot. In between the time they sent the telegram and the time the person get there . . . they done forgot all about them" (19). His experiences have also taught him that there is no one place black people can call home. For now, at least, they must go where the track leads them. The lines are laid, the rules set; neither can be bent. Unable to force circumstances in the direction they want, blacks must wait for the right moment and then seize it—they must catch the right train or wait patiently. There are thousands of miles of track, and sooner or later one will lead to their destination. In the meantime, they must make their homes wherever they find themselves.

Although Boy Willie and Wining Boy want to return south, their reasons are widely different—the uncle seeks personal spiritual renewal, while the nephew yearns for racial authentication. Boy Willie's desire to be master on a farm where his entire family had been slaves is a passionate crusade of mythic proportions. This proposal—to own a farm in the South where attitudes have not changed much since the Civil War—is so full of effrontery as to be almost outrageous. But it is not without merit. However cosmic his quest, there is a pragmatic aspect to it. Instead of migrating north to live as a third-class citizen on the outskirts of a resentful society, he wants to stay home and do the work that generations of his race have done before him—this time as an owner, not as a slave. By the end of the play he may not have the money to make the payment on the farm, but he takes a far more significant step toward establishing the identity of his family as truly free black men and women—free from the psychological and emotional shackles of the past, free from the incubus of their white owners, and free from the dissension that threatened to sever them.

Boy Willie shares the same individual streak that motivated Troy Maxson, the same rebellious impulse that drove Levee. They will not allow him to flee his home in the South. His is not the acquiescent way of Avery; not for him the droppings from the white man's table, the leftovers thrown to keep him quiet and submissive. He too can trace his mythological lineage to Eshu, the trickster deity who rails against the status quo and the rigidity of rule and order, preferring the freedom of individual will. When the white woman buying his watermelons wants to know if they are sweet, his reply—"where we grow these watermelons we put sugar in the ground"—is as slick and quick-witted as the retorts of his cultural ancestor, Brer Rabbit.

This passionate determination to make his own way springs from a deep conviction that he is not inferior to the white man—he will not stay at the bottom of the social ladder despite the forces conspiring to keep him there. Unlike his sister, Berniece, he refuses to capitulate to the weight of circumstances: "I ain't gonna take my life and throw it away at the bottom." Nor does he need to go north to find his identity. He is the scion of a proud heritage, the bearer of a standard handed down by several generations of a family that refused to die; a family that struggled through slavery and sharecropping and survived into freedom. For too long they have been at the bottom of the wheel of fortune. Now, in one audacious move, he will spin the wheel and reverse the situation. At this moment, he feels a special kinship with his father, Boy Charles, for he knows the act that brought the piano into their house was an act of daring that altered forever the way in which this family could look at itself. It transformed their identity from slaves and sharecroppers to free men and women unafraid to die for their freedom. Admonishing Berniece for being ashamed of the piano and for not telling her daughter, Maretha, about its history, Boy Willie says she should throw a party on the anniversary of the day the piano came into their home.

In a way, the four generations—from the first Boy Willie to the present Boy Willie—that were involved with the piano constitute the childhood of the Charles family as free people. The moment the elder Boy Willie (Boy Willie's great-grandfather) carved the images on the piano, he took the first step toward freedom, for he denied his owner the right or power to separate his family. That act also gave a group of dispossessed people an heirloom to call their own, a precious relic to keep them together. That the piano almost disrupts the family is only part of the teething process as they toddle toward freedom. The next important step came when Boy Charles took the piano from the Sutter household—a symbolic break for freedom that cost him his life. Now, Boy Willie is preparing for the deed that will enable his family finally to come of age—the ex-slaves will become owners of the farm that enslaved them. By doing it he will complete the work begun by his great-grandfather. Reinforcing the image of a family in the infancy and childhood of its freedom is the fact that these three men all have childish names—Boy Willie (the elder), Boy Charles, and Boy Willie. Wining Boy also belongs to this group, for his decision to return to the South is another step toward freedom— an assertion that he will no longer run from the South but return to claim it as his home.

Racial redress lies across a mine-field of intolerance and inequity, but Boy Willie is well girded for the battle. He has the Charles spirit, handed down to him by his father and mother. He also has the piano—a legacy from his father and great-grandfather that he can use as collateral to free himself from the oppression of the past: "I was born to a time of fire. The world ain't wanted no part of me. . . . But my mama ain't birthed me for nothing. So what I got to do? I got to mark my passing on the road. Just like you write on a tree, 'Boy Willie was here.' That's all I'm trying to do with that piano. Trying to put my mark on the road. Like my daddy done. My heart say for me to sell that piano and get me some land so I can make a life for myself to live in my own way" (93–94). The fact that he does not get the piano is doubly significant, for it suggests, first, that Berniece's—and, by extension, the Charles family's—mental and psychological freedom are more important than the act of completing the circle and taking over the Sutter farm; and second, that the piano itself is more valuable than the farm.[7]

From the moment Boy Willie storms into this house—through his arguments with Berniece, his bantering with Lymon, his aggressive advances on Grace, and his final fight with Sutter's ghost—there is a fiery quality to him. Poised to do battle with everyone, he sees himself very much as a man for his time—unwilling to suffer any more indignities, he will seize control of his own fate. Here again the similarities to Levee are evident—both are in their thirties, aggressive, and disinclined to settle for crumbs. And while their similarities are noble, the differences between them are crucial. Though he has had his share of adversity, Boy Willie has no wish to strike out blindly at the white race; nor will he pander to a white man to get what he wants. The most important distinction is that Boy Willie does not reject his cultural legacy. In wanting to sell the piano he is merely attempting to use his heritage to create a new beginning, confident that his father would have done the same: "If my daddy had seen where he could have traded that piano in for some land of his own, it wouldn't be sitting up here now." Thus, in wanting to sell the piano, he does not reject all that the piano symbolizes; rather, he acknowledges that the past can provide creative solutions for the future. At the same time, he seeks to validate, in a practical way, the sufferings of his ancestors, to ensure that their sacrifices were not in vain.

Unfortunately, in attempting to do this he is also playing into the hands of the mysterious white man who is trying to acquire musical instruments from black people. By selling the piano to him, Boy Willie would be trading the source of his family's power and identity, however honorable and even admirable his intentions may be. So he must be brought to the realization that the piano is more than a "piece of wood" to be used as collateral; that it is a sacred vault in which are embalmed the memories and sacrifices of his family; that it is indeed worthy of the annual celebration he suggested for it. For her part, Berniece must realize that it is not a millstone around her neck; that it is more than a repository of the grief that beset her family; that those who died for it did so that their descendants might live. The dilemma is amplified because both actions—to sell or not to sell— possess potentially positive and negative ramifications. The solution lies in brother and sister being brought to some understanding of each other's point of view.

Before they can achieve this realization, they have to undergo the purgation that will banish the obsessive ghosts of the past. By feuding bitterly over the piano, they have repudiated its essential function—to keep this family together. In their hands it has become a divisive force, sundering sibling bonds and preventing the Charles family from transcending its past and taking the final step to freedom. As if to underscore the ominous presence of this past and the fact that the bonds of slavery have not been completely severed, Sutter's ghost freely roams the Charles household. As long as this is a house divided, they will be enslaved by the destructive elements of their past and their former owner who will not leave. It is time to exorcise the evil spirits and let the healing spirit of the past flow through this house. Avery offers a Christian blessing and exorcism, but they need something more, for Christian rites are insufficient to dispel the ghosts of Christian oppressors. Besides, Boy Willie, like Levee and Loomis, has lost his faith in the power of Christianity. Disenchanted with the white man's God, he has found his own way: "That's when I discovered the power of death. See, a nigger that ain't afraid to die is the worse kind of nigger for the white man. He can't hold that power over you. That's what I learned when I killed that cat. I got the power of death too. I can command him. I can call him up. The white man don't like to see that. He don't like for you to stand up and look him square in the eye and say, 'I got it too.' Then he got to deal with you square up" (88).[8]

With a strength born of this knowledge, Boy Willie engages in a deadly struggle with Sutter's ghost. In a cosmic battle with the devil who has haunted and controlled this family for generations, he launches the truly daring act that will free them forever. This is the final round in a fight that his father and the ghosts of the Yellow Dog have waged for a long time. For years, these ghosts have wreaked vengeance on the white men who terrorized the black community in Sunflower—every time a black man was killed, the white man responsible died mysteriously, usually by falling down a well. But the ghosts were more than vigilante spirits. As Wining Boy discovered when he sought their advice at the railroad crossing, they were also sources of strength and inspiration for dispirited blacks in need of renewed energy for the daily struggles that faced them. Sutter is the last oppressor left. In a reversal of the pattern in which white men were ostensibly killed by the ghosts, Sutter is now a ghost and it is up to the living to banish him forever.

The importance of the legend lies in its symbolic suggestion that solutions to present problems lie in the past, that dead ancestors are perhaps so potent because they have all the answers, are within reach of the living, and beyond harm. Just as Loomis's vision of his dead ancestors unloosed the first shackles of his cultural enslavement, so the actions of the ghosts of the Yellow Dog are a continual exhortation to the Charles family that passivity is precisely what keeps them chained to the white man. As if in response, Boy Willie flings himself into a life and death struggle for what is his. But he cannot do it by himself. Myriad forces must join in the battle, for this fight is not for one person, or one family, but a whole race of people.

As her brother wrestles with Sutter's ghost, Berniece is suddenly aware of what she must do. She knows that the piano contains the spirits of her ancestors, and it is to them that she turns. Like a high priestess on a shamanic journey of redemption, she walks to the piano and summons a benediction from its depths. In a final moment of reconciliation she fashions a spiritual from her memories, a song born in an ancient culture from which the winds of exorcism will rise and then gather force as they blend with the hallowed spirits of her dead relatives.

Although the spirituals were influenced by Christianity, they are more African in form and substance than has often been realized. Like the ring shout, they were an important part of ancestral ceremonies (Stuckey 27). It is thus fitting that Berniece turns to the spiritual, for what she most needs now are her ancestors—the whole community must band together for the final battle.[9] So she calls out the names of her dead family—Mama Berniece, Mama Esther, Papa Boy Charles, and Mama Ola. At this moment of spiritual invocation, time and space are suspended; past and present come together, and the ancestral spirits surge forth from the piano to bless this house that they built. At last, brother and sister find themselves on the same side, united against a common enemy, bonded in a common destiny. This is the lesson that the piano teaches them: only as a united family can they transpose the discordant rhythms of bondage into the harmony of full freedom.

In Wilson's family plays—*Joe Turner, Fences, The Piano Lesson*—he has cast a young girl in an important role. She is the binding one, the link that keeps family members from irrevocable separation, the person who will perpetuate the blessings and transcendence achieved by her family. In *Joe Turner,* it was through Zonia that the bonds between Loomis and Martha would be preserved; as the daughter of a born-again African and a Christian evangelist, she represented a new generation of Afro-Christians. In *Fences,* Raynell kept Troy and Rose together until they arrived at a new understanding of their relationship. In the final scene, she helped Cory sing Troy's song, and in that moment of harmony the son found the strength and grace to forgive his father and be reconciled with his spirit. At the end of *The Piano Lesson,* Boy Willie tells Berniece that unless she lets Maretha play the piano, both he and Sutter's ghost will be back. The young girl is thus charged with preserving the newfound ties between sister and brother. In her innocent hands, the piano will fill their house with its song of freedom, and its music will be a touchstone for the daily process of reappraisals and renegotiations by these people struggling for survival.

This play is, therefore, a depiction of a new journey, or, perhaps, a new direction in the odyssey of African Americans in the twentieth century. Contained in Boy Willie's resolve to stay south as a free landowner is a promise to sanctify the lives and labors of his ancestors. It is an assertion that slavery is now over and the land belongs to whoever can buy it and work on it. But first he must understand the communal aspect of his mission—that the task he undertakes is not an individual venture but an endeavor made possible by the efforts of those who went before; that their toil commissioned the journey on which he now embarks. In signing a pact with Berniece, Boy Willie acknowledges his debt to his ancestors and realizes that the heirlooms of his family are not mere collateral to be pawned but sacred totems to be carried into the battles ahead. And in this covenant, Berniece finds the strength to confront the agony of the past so that she can face the freedom that the future promises.

CONCLUSION

These four plays cover a period of about fifty years. Their chronological sequence—from the 1911 of *Joe Turner* to the 1957 of *Fences*—spans a half century of struggle that grudgingly yielded only a few concessions to black Americans in their quest for self-authentication. The prevailing sense that the changes came very slowly—a full century to achieve the recognition promised by the Emancipation Proclamation—is sifted through the themes of migration and separation, which stretch the backdrops of the plays beyond their immediate locales in the twentieth century to the eras of slavery and Reconstruction. The theme of reunion propels them further back, into the real and mythological dimensions of the characters' African pasts.

I have chosen to consider the plays in the order in which they were written mainly because this sequence permitted me also to study Wilson's growth as an artist dealing with the same themes in four different plays. It is clear that with each succeeding work his sense of the themes of separation, migration, and reunion grew keener. In *Ma Rainey,* they are very much in the background, explicated through the use of stories and narrative dialogue. In *Fences,* separation is an integral part of the central conflict between Troy and his family and the society that surrounds them. In the background, a fence becomes a symbol of the conflict and the theme of separation. In *Joe Turner,* Wilson's most complex play, there is a criss-crossing of all three themes as they vitalize the spiritual odysseys of the characters. Reunion finds a deep, mythological signification here and in *The Piano Lesson,* where the symbol is much more in the foreground and central to the action than in *Fences.* This is not to impute any value judgments to the plays—that one or more are better than the others—but simply to suggest that these particular themes are more intrinsic to the structure of the later plays.

Although the spiritual transcendence that marks the end of *Fences, Joe Turner,* and *The Piano Lesson* does not occur in quite the same way in *Ma Rainey*—Wilson's darkest play—where we are left with the devastating sight of a man destroyed by his own angst, the heroic flavor of Levee's pursuit of self-empowerment is the prelude to an investigation—in the other plays—of the warrior spirit that seeks to thwart the destructive rhythms of racial prejudice. This spirit fuels the actions of Troy, Loomis, and Boy Willie as they cut an individual swath through the underbrush of a clogging white society, and it elevates them into the realm of tragic heroes. Although the deaths of classical European tragedy are absent here, several characters suffer physical and mental anguish—Levee, Troy, Rose, Cory, Loomis, Martha, Mattie, Berniece, Wining Boy. Through their epic struggles they transcend their mortal plight, affording us a view that all tragedy offers—a glimpse of the indomitable human spirit.

The search for cultural identity and self-affirmation is linked to the question of survival. All the characters are engaged, at various levels of intensity, in a fight for survival, for their struggle to be accepted as free citizens is actually a battle against the forces that threaten to destroy them. To survive, they seek self-reinvention in cultural and mythological dimensions—Loomis rejects his identity as a Christian preacher because it undermined his self-worth and finds succor in his renewed identity as an African; Martha, on the other hand, discovers a haven within Christian Evangelism. Bertha negotiates a comfortable path between African and Christian traditions. Thwarted by a hostile society in his roles as breadwinner, father, and husband, Troy attains self-affirmation in the same African phallocentric trickster tradition that empowers Levee and Boy Willie. Rose rediscovers her identity as a nurturing mother, commemorating a communal African custom, and Avery's desire to be a preacher is a similar quest for self-validation within a community. Having banished the destructive ghosts of her past, Berniece can experience renewed strength in a spiritual communion with her family, past and present. Boy Willie reorders the universe, Wining Boy pursues the lost spirit of his blues in the South, and Lyons encounters that spirit in the North. And the oracular voice of Bynum, the People Binder, continues to attest and affirm the authenticity of their cultural resurrections.

With each decade, as they reinvent themselves to survive the urban jungle of twentieth-century America, blacks seek new ways to affirm their self-worth. After three centuries of humiliation were followed by broken promises and denied opportunities in the Reconstruction and post-Reconstruction eras, they were in great need of a healing process. Their continued oppression in the twentieth century caused further rifts among them—physically, as they simply left each other and escaped in search of better conditions, and sociopsychologically, as hatred and alienation precipitated communal fragmentation. With white America unwilling to render reparation, blacks began to heal themselves through a communal renewal with their roots—self-affirmation within the cultural fraternity. Thus reunion and reinvention center round their African origins, their southern roots, their ancestors, and each other. It is significant that the only play without this sense of reunion—*Ma Rainey*—does not have the family at the heart of its action. It is worth noting, however, the strong communal bond between Ma Rainey and her sidemen, whose playing of the blues is a constant reunion with their cultural roots. The introduction of Ma's nephew, Sylvester, to the group heightens this familial sense. Levee remains outside the community, and his refusal to join the circle is partly responsible for his downfall.

The characters' need to belong to a community springs from the sense of rootlessness that slavery engendered. Music—gospel, spirituals, blues, and jazz—is their strongest common bond, for it links them to all their roots: slavery, the South, and Africa. It is an integral part of the reunion they seek and therefore has a crucial function in these plays. Without the music they would be a disjointed bunch of people clawing for a social foothold. Through it they can take collective heart in their ability to survive. For better or worse, the music is a daily replaying of brutal personal and communal history, and its "near-tragic, near-comic lyricism" permits a transcendence of those experiences, imbuing their lives with meaning and purpose. It, more than anything, gives them an enormous sense of cultural identity and self-worth, for it is a continuous reminder that they are not just a group of ex-slaves but African-American artists.

NOTES

Introduction

1. The entire tale and its implications are discussed by Stuckey in *Slave Culture*, 4–6.

2. In India there is constant evidence of this confluence of the religious with the material, not only in the myriad festive pageants that swarm the streets to mingle there with the daily routine of life but also in the refusal to take any significant step—weddings, business deals, travels—without first ensuring that the time is astrologically propitious.

Chapter 1: *Ma Rainey's Black Bottom*

1. The generally accepted date of the beginning of the Harlem Renaissance is 1917. "James Weldon Johnson informally inaugurated the *movement* with his publication of *Fifty Years and Other Poems* in 1917" (Southern 396). But it took a few years before black musicians were recorded. Mark White mentions "Kid" Ory's two titles for the "obscure Sunshine label" in Los Angeles in 1921 (21). In 1917 and 1922, the Original Dixieland Jazz Band and the New Orleans Rhythm Kings—both white bands—had recordings; but King Oliver's 1923 recording was the first black jazz to reach a wide audience.

2. In 1927, a show with which he was touring became stranded in Kansas City. For a year he played the piano in a movie theater pit and then joined Walter Page's Blue Devils orchestra. In 1929 he joined Bennie Moten's orchestra. It was only in 1935 that Basie started his own orchestra. But his introduction to Kansas City began in 1927, and he was the definitive exponent of the Kansas City swinging style. More details are available in Eileen Southern's *Music of Black Americans*, 382–85.

3. Southern's description of the evolution of swing underscores the

importance of the blues: "Inevitably the blues became the basic material used in this kind of performance [i.e., jam sessions or cutting contests]. Its structure was fixed—the standard twelve-bar form and prescribed harmonic patterns—and it was familiar to all jazzmen. Moreover the basic simplicity of the blues lent itself well to reshaping and elaboration. Blues could be handled to fit any mood; played fast, it generated excitement, and played slowly, it was as melancholy as could be desired" (383).

4. *Griots* were African minstrel historians who recited the historical events of their tribes or sang songs of praise or exhortation (Southern 9–10). See also Robert Palmer's *Deep Blues*, 27.

5. This is significant, for, as we have already perceived in his mythological lineage, Levee also has some of the admirable qualities of classical tragic heroes that stemmed from their hubris; in particular, the defiant attitude that challenged the gods and the status quo, refusing to accept the fate that was decreed for them. While this attitude led to physical destruction, the triumph of tragedy was in spiritual transcendence.

6. Ma Rainey and W. C. Handy are generally acknowledged as the first professional blues musicians. Although they did not invent the blues, how each of them happened upon it is related by Palmer in *Deep Blues*, 44–45.

7. About the piano and guitar in the rhythm section Jerry Coker says that "the function of the pianist and that of the guitarist are, for all practical purposes, identical. Therefore, it is common to see rhythm sections which use either piano or guitar, but not both instruments, as they will collide as two drummers would, unless their functions, by prior agreement, are sufficiently different that they do not collide. Count Basie (pianist) solved the problem in his band by having his guitarist (Freddy Green) strum in steady quarter-note valued chords, while Basie used a very sparse left hand and played light, melodic figures in the right hand" (39). Thus, Cutler's guitar probably played chord changes while keeping time, supported by Slow Drag's bass line; Toledo's piano would have "copped changes," which means playing staccato chords at odd intervals or with embellished riffs (short melodic phrases that suggest improvisation).

8. In *Joe Turner,* this sense of nonentity in the large city is evident in Jeremy's brushes with the law.

9. This process is extensively documented in several books, among them *Blues People: The Negro Experience in White America and the Music*

That Developed from It, by LeRoi Jones, and *The White Man's Burden: Historical Origins of Racism in the United States,* by W. D. Jordan.

10. According to Eugene Genovese, "the Alabama Baptist Association at its annual meeting in 1850 called for greater efforts to instruct the slaves: 'Intelligent masters with the light of experience before them will regard the communication of sound religious instruction as the truest economy and the most efficient police and as tending to the greatest utility, with regard to every interest involved'" (189).

11. Palmer writes of the great Delta bluesman Robert Johnson, who was considered to be in league with the devil. According to his relatives, he sold his soul to the devil at a backcountry crossroads in return for his talent (113). This gave rise to the lore that the blues comes from the devil. The interesting corollary to this is the implication that the devil inspired the music that provided the black man with a way to deal with his inhuman treatment at the hands of Christian white men.

12. It is significant that, like other valuable blacks, Levee will end up in jail.

Chapter 2: *Fences*

1. All these cases are documented in such books as *Desegregation and the Law,* by Albert P. Blaustein and Clarence Clyde Ferguson, Jr.

2. Civil Rights Act of 1957, 71 STAT. 635; 42 U.S.C. 1975 (1952). Blaustein and Ferguson maintain that its primary purpose was to "investigate allegations . . . that certain citizens of the United States are being deprived of their right to vote and have their vote counted by reason of their color, race, religion, or national origin" (287).

3. "Walking blues" has created the idiom of the "walking" or "traveling" bass line. Thus, not only is the lyric significant in this format, but the actual structure of the bass line suggests continuous movement.

4. In his book *Only the Ball Was White,* Robert Peterson discusses the barnstorming life of black baseball players who traveled in unbelievably difficult conditions just for the chance to continue playing.

5. Several players and writers have testified that black players were talented enough to play in the majors. This body of opinion is well documented in such books as *Only the Ball Was White,* by Peterson, and *Get That Nigger Off the Field,* by Art Rust, Jr.

6. Although Rose tries to persuade Troy to admit that he was too old

to play in the majors, he knows it was his color, not his age, that barred him. Peterson suggests that Satchel Paige was close to fifty years old when he signed with the Cleveland Indians (131).

7. It is worth remembering that the sixties only brought to fruition the cultural and political seeds planted in the fifties, as W. T. Lhamon, Jr., argues so ably in his book *Deliberate Speed: The Origins of a Cultural Style in the American 1950s.*

8. Levee's rejection of the blues is filled with scorn and mockery. Troy, on the other hand, is only resentful about the lack of opportunity in his career. His attitude toward athletics is filled with bitterness, not disrespect or scorn. By keeping Cory away from athletics he is merely trying to protect his son. This bitterness prevents him from fulfilling his potential, but it does not destroy him in the way Levee is destroyed.

Chapter 3: *Joe Turner's Come and Gone*

1. Historians give 1915 as the year in which the mass movement really started. World War I had slowed the immigration from Europe and Northern employers were forced to depend on domestic labor.

2. The organization was founded to provide assistance to new arrivals from the South, to help workers prepare for jobs in industry, and to convince white employers to open job opportunities for blacks.

3. Two dollars is what Seth charges for room and board (including meals) for a week.

4. There is an interesting parallel here to the ancient Jews of the Old Testament, whose freedom from Pharaoh also meant rootlessness—wandering in the wilderness for forty years. The great migration of blacks started in the second decade of the twentieth century, forty years before the events of the fifties gave them full citizenship. Both races spent several centuries in bondage, both faced decades of rootlessness, and both continued to be persecuted because of their race.

5. Genovese writes that "slaves and ex-slaves . . . described the conjurers' power over the quarters. Ex-slaves often identified the conjurers as having been African-born, but possibly those African-born slaves who still remained in late antebellum times came to be thought of as natural conjurers. The blacks believed that only blacks, especially those born with a caul, had the secret power and that it was somehow a gift of their African heritage" (218).

6. Siva also embodies in himself all these apparent oppositions; he is creator, preserver, and destroyer.

7. Sprinkling salt is an old superstition to wards off ghosts (Puckett 143).

8. The Christian baptismal rite has interesting parallels in African ritual. Stuckey writes that an invariable element in various African tribal rituals was a visit to a body of "living" water. "Thus, Yorubas, Ashantis, and Dahomeans would easily have identified with the pilgrimage to the Mill Pond for a [baptismal] ceremony that was heavily influenced by Bakongo religious ritual" (34).

9. Palmer describes it thus: "Village music making in Senegambia involves drumming, hand clapping, and group singing in call and response form; usually an improvising vocal soloist is answered by a chorus singing a repeating refrain in unison" (27).

10. Perhaps more than any other scene in the play, this one needs to be seen for its essential effect to be clear. Wilson's stage directions regarding the juba should be followed explicitly—the dance must build to a frenzy. Only then can the rest of the scene be effective, for the body slaps and rhythmic movements of the juba have a kind of table-tapping, seance-like effect and are partly responsible for calling up the vision that seizes Loomis. Further, if the shouting, clapping, and stamping reach a crescendo, Loomis will be forced to scream his anger in order to stop the dance, forcing him into a frenzy, and that energy will lead him first into the Pentecostal trance and then into the vision of the bones. Lastly, it is important that the frenzied first half of the scene be rhythmically contrasted against the highly patterned call and response second half. The fluctuating percussive effects thus created reflect the essentially African nature of black American music.

11. There is a symbolic parallel between the trapped pigeons and black people, for both were promised freedom and both find themselves sold for profit—the pigeons to Bynum, blacks in the exploitative marketplace of the industrial North.

12. This same attitude vindicated the imperialistic designs of most of Western Europe's monarchies—British, Dutch, Spanish, Portuguese. All these colonial-minded civilizations brandished their Christian faith like banners as they imposed their European cultures on Asian, African, and South American nations. What makes this ironic is that Christianity was essentially a non-Western religion embraced by Westerners and used as a weapon to subdue other non-Westerners.

13. It is important to note that Genovese also suggests that while the Nietzschean view of Christianity "contains an element of truth, [it] remains a one-sided and therefore superficial judgement upon a religion

that carried the ideas of spiritual equality and of the freedom of the will and soul across Europe and the world. . . . To see only that side is to surrender all chance to understand the contribution of Afro-American Christianity to the survival and mobilization of black America. . . . From its beginnings Christianity has precariously balanced submission to authority against the courage of the individual will. In a special way, fraught with consequences for the oppressed of that time and after, it has not been able to maintain this balance without great violence, for it has never been able to impose permanent restraint on the socially subversive impulses of the will" (163–64).

14. Confrontation does not mean that every black person should undergo slavery in order to be free of its stigma. That there are many ways to achieve this purgation is one of the messages of *The Piano Lesson*.

Chapter 4: *The Piano Lesson*

1. Most of these events are recorded and discussed by Eileen Southern in *The Music of Black Americans: A History* and by Henry Sampson in *Blacks in Blackface*.

2. Although *Fences* is set in 1957, the migration that Troy and Bono talk about occurred many years earlier—probably long before the thirties.

3. In 1936, with Jesse Owens's success at the Berlin Olympics, athletics opened the second avenue for blacks to excel at the national and international levels.

4. Although their original roots are in Africa, the new roots of African Americans are in the South. As they started to move away from the plantations and discovered that life in the great North was a broken promise, one of the places they could look back at longingly was the South. Obviously, all blacks did not feel that way; but Boy Willie and Wining Boy do, albeit for different reasons.

5. It is significant that Doaker, Wining Boy, Boy Willie, and Lymon have all served sentences on Parchman Farm.

6. In many cultures, the eating of food eases tensions and clears the air for rapprochement, bringing warring factions together. The kitchen, therefore, seems the right place to grapple with conflicts that have deep cultural roots. But the final resolutions are beyond the control of Bertha or Doaker; they must be effected by Loomis and by Boy Willie and Berniece. Significantly, they occur in the parlor, not the kitchen.

7. This is not to suggest that Boy Willie loses the farm. After all, he

did say to Berniece that had she been putting the piano to good use he would have had to find another way to get the money. Besides, the piano would only account for a third of the money. He already has the other two-thirds. There is every reason to suppose that, enterprising as he is, Boy Willie will find another way. But, of course, that is not within this play.

8. Like Levee, Boy Willie seems to be drawn toward death. But while Levee's self-destructive streak courts death, finding it attractive, Boy Willie seeks its power as a way to survive. In the ultimate analysis, Boy Willie reaches for life, Levee for death.

9. Stuckey writes: "The repetition of stanzas as the dancers circled around and around with ever greater acceleration reinforced and deepened the spirit of familial attachment, drawing within the ancestral orbit slaves who may not have known either a father or a mother, their involvement being an extension of that of others, the circle symbolizing the unbroken unity of the community" (27).

Levine also discusses the fact that spirituals play an important part in the continuation of the community and that their overriding antiphonal structure is related to the call and response nature of African music (33).

WORKS CITED

Blaustein, Albert P., and Clarence Clyde Ferguson, Jr. *Desegregation and the Law: The Meaning and Effect of the School Segregation Cases*. 2d ed. rev. New York: Vintage Books/Random House, 1962.

Ching, Mei-Ling. "Two Notes on August Wilson: Wrestling against History." *Theatre* (Summer/Fall 1988): 70–71.

Coker, Jerry. *Listening to Jazz*. New York: Prentice-Hall, 1978.

Eliade, Mircea. *Shamanism: Archaic Techniques of Ecstasy*. Trans. Willard R. Trask. New York: Pantheon, 1964.

Ellison, Ralph. *Shadow and Act*. New York: Random House, 1964.

Foner, Eric. *Reconstruction: America's Unfinished Revolution*. New York: Harper & Row, 1988.

Genovese, Eugene D. *Roll, Jordan, Roll*. New York: Vintage Books/Random House, 1976.

Glover, Margaret E. "Two Notes on August Wilson: The Songs of a Marked Man." *Theatre* (Summer/Fall 1988): 69–70.

Grant, Robert B. *The Black Man Comes to the City: A Documentary Account from the Great Migration to the Great Depression, 1915 to 1930*. Chicago: Nelson-Hall, 1972.

Harrison, Paul Carter. *August Wilson: Three Plays*. Pittsburgh: University of Pittsburgh Press, 1991.

Jones, LeRoi. *Blues People: The Negro Experience in White America and the Music That Developed from It*. New York: Morrow Quill Paperbacks, 1963.

Jordan, Winthrop D. *The White Man's Burden: Historical Origins of Racism in the United States*. 1974; New York: Oxford University Press, 1976.

Kautsky, Karl. *Foundations of Christianity*. Trans. Henry F. Mins. New York: Russell & Russell, 1953.

Levine, Lawrence W. *Black Culture and Black Consciousness: Afro-American Folk Thought from Slavery to Freedom.* New York: Oxford University Press, 1977.

Lhamon, W. T., Jr. *Deliberate Speed: The Origins of a Cultural Style in the American 1950s.* Washington, D.C.: Smithsonian Institution Press, 1990.

Moyers, Bill. "August Wilson's America: A Conversation with Bill Moyers." *American Theatre* (June 1989): 13–17, 54.

Odugbesan, Clara. "Femininity in Yoruba Religious Art." In *Man in Africa.* Ed. Mary Douglas and Phyllis M. Kaberry. London: Tavistock Publications, 1969.

Palmer, Robert. *Deep Blues.* 1981; New York: Penguin, 1982.

Peterson, Robert. *Only the Ball Was White.* New York: Prentice-Hall, 1970.

Puckett, Newbell Niles. *Folk Beliefs of the Southern Negro.* Chapel Hill: University of North Carolina Press, 1926.

Rust, Art, Jr. *Get That Nigger Off the Field.* New York: Grosset & Dunlap, 1974.

Sampson, Henry T. *Blacks in Blackface: A Source Book on Early Black Musical Shows.* Metuchen, N.J.: Scarecrow Press, 1980.

Southern, Eileen. *The Music of Black Americans: A History.* 2d ed. New York: W. W. Norton, 1983.

Stearns, Marshall. *The Story of Jazz.* New York: Oxford University Press, 1956.

Stuckey, Sterling. *Slave Culture: Nationalist Theory and the Foundations of Black America.* New York: Oxford University Press, 1987.

White, Mark. *The Observer's Book of Jazz.* London: Frederick Warne, 1978.

Wilson, August. *Ma Rainey's Black Bottom.* New York: Plume/New American Library, 1985.

———. *Fences.* New York: Plume/New American Library, 1986.

———. *Joe Turner's Come and Gone.* New York: Plume/New American Library, 1988.

———. *The Piano Lesson.* New York: Dutton/Penguin, 1990.

Woodward, C. Vann. *The Strange Career of Jim Crow.* 2d ed. rev. New York: Oxford University Press, 1966.

INDEX

KIM PEREIRA teaches acting and dramatic literature at Illinois State University. Originally from India, he came to the United States in 1986 and received a Ph.D. in theater from Florida State University. An actor and director, he lives in Bloomington, Illinois, with his wife, Lorraine; his daughter, Liesl Antonia Dominique; and his son, Kieran Blake Ashlyn.